Work Overload!

Redesigning Jobs to Minimize Stress and Burnout

Also Available from ASQ Quality Press:

Performance Measurement Explained: Designing and Implementing Your State-of-the-Art System
Bjørn Andersen and Tom Fagerhaug

Bringing Business Ethics to Life: Achieving Corporate Social Responsibility
Bjørn Andersen

Transformational Leadership: Creating Organizations of Meaning
Stephen Hacker and Tammy Roberts

The Trust Imperative: Performance Improvement Through Productive Relationships
Stephen Hacker and Marsha Willard

Making Change Work: Practical Tools for Overcoming Human Resistance to Change
Brien Palmer

The Recipe for Simple Business Improvement
David W. Till

The Synergy of One: Creating High-Performing Sustainable Organizations through Integrated Performance Leadership
Michael J. Dreikorn

Certified Quality Manager Handbook: Second Edition
Duke Okes and Russell T. Westcott, editors

To request a complimentary catalog of ASQ Quality Press publications, call 800-248-1946, or visit our website at http://qualitypress.asq.org.

Work Overload!

Redesigning Jobs to Minimize Stress and Burnout

Frank M. Gryna

ASQ Quality Press
Milwaukee, Wisconsin

American Society for Quality, Quality Press, Milwaukee 53203
© 2004 by Frank M. Gryna
All rights reserved. Published 2004
Printed in the United States of America

12 11 10 09 08 07 06 05 04   5 4 3 2 1

Library of Congress Cataloging-in-Publication Data

Gryna, Frank M.
  Work overload! : redesigning jobs to minimize stress and burnout / by
Frank M. Gryna.
      p. cm.
  ISBN 0-87389-624-6 (pbk. : alk. paper)
  1. Job stress. 2. Work and family. 3. Work—Psychological aspects. 4.
Work—Physiological aspects. I. Title.

  HF5548.85.G79 2004
  158.7'2--dc22
                                          2003028150
  ISBN 0-87389-624-6

, Publisher: William A. Tony
Acquisitions Editor: Annemieke Hytinen
Project Editor: Paul O'Mara
Production Administrator: Randall Benson
Special Marketing Representative: Matt Meinholtz

ASQ Mission: The American Society for Quality advances individual,
organizational, and community excellence worldwide through learning,
quality improvement, and knowledge exchange.

Attention Bookstores, Wholesalers, Schools, and Corporations: ASQ
Quality Press books, videotapes, audiotapes, and software are available at
quantity discounts with bulk purchases for business, educational, or
instructional use.
For information, please contact ASQ Quality Press at 800-248-1946, or
write to ASQ Quality Press, P.O. Box 3005, Milwaukee, WI 53201-3005.

To place orders or to request a free copy of the ASQ Quality Press
Publications Catalog, including ASQ membership information, call
800-248-1946. Visit our Web site at www.asq.org or
http://qualitypress.asq.org.

∞ Printed on acid-free paper

Quality Press
600 N. Plankinton Avenue
Milwaukee, Wisconsin 53203
Call toll free 800-248-1946
Fax 414-272-1734
www.asq.org
http://qualitypress.asq.org
http://standardsgroup.asq.org
E-mail: authors@asq.org

AMERICAN SOCIETY
FOR QUALITY

With love, I dedicate this book to my family: my wife, Dee, our daughter, Wendy Esslinger, and her husband; Perry, our son, Derek Gryna, and his wife, Barbara; our son Gary Gryna, and his wife, Dina; and the cavalcade of grandchildren: Jason, Sarah, and Elizabeth Esslinger; Wesley, William, and Whitney Gryna; and Emily and Samuel Gryna.

Table of Contents

List of Figures and Tables . . . . *xi*

Preface . . . . *xiii*

Acknowledgments . . . . *xv*

Chapter 1   How Serious Is the Work Overload Issue? . . .   **1**
Who Suffers From Work Overload?   1
The Warning Signs of Work Overload   3
To What Extent Is Work Overload Common?   4
What Are the Reasons for Work Overload?   6
How Do We React to Work Overload?   8
Work Overload – Self-Assessment   9
Viewpoints of This Book   10
Summary – Three Key Points   11

Chapter 2   What Are the Causes of Work Overload? **13**
The Ten Contributing Causes   13
Is Work Overload a Heavy Hitter to Job Satisfaction? . . .   17
Summary – Three Key Points   17

Chapter 3   Why Study Waste in a Process? **19**
Do We Change the Work or Change the Person?   19
All Work Is Done in a Process   20
What Are the Forms of Waste in a Process?   21
Who Will Do the Analyses to Eliminate Process Waste?   . .   23
How Can We Be Sure That Savings in Process
    Waste Will Help to Reduce Work Overload   25

Analyzing for Waste in a Process   25
Reality – Staff Low, Add People, but Never Enough . . .   33
Summary – Three Key Points   34

**Chapter 4   How Can We Redesign Work at the Process
Level to Eliminate Work Overload?** **35**
Process Waste and Work Overload   35
Redesign at the Process Level – Radical and
    Incremental Change   36
Guidelines for Redesign of Processes   38
Summary – Three Key Points   42

**Chapter 5   How Do the Mental Demands of Work
Contribute to Work Overload?** **43**
Long Hours + Excessive Mental Demands = Work
    Overload   44
Mental Demands and Job Content   44
Mental Demands Caused by Job Content   45
Mental Demands and Poor Management Practices   48
Summary – Three Key Points   50

**Chapter 6   How Can We Redesign Work
at the Job Level?** **53**
Analysis of Job Characteristics   54
Analysis for Mental Demands   56
Analysis for Self-Control   61
Checklist for Manufacturing Sector   62
Checklist for Service Sector   68
Redesign for Work and Family Life – Case Examples . . .   75
Summary – Three Key Points   77

Chapter 7   How Do We Match Work to People? **79**
Why Middle Managers Spend Most of Their
    Day on "People Problems"   79
Work Overload and Selection of Personnel   80
What to Do When Personnel Requisitions
    Cannot Be Filled   84
Work Overload and Training of Employees   88
Work Overload and Retention of Key Employees   89
Summary – Three Key Points   92

**Chapter 8   How Do We Achieve Participation
and Empowerment of Employees to Reduce
Work Overload?** **95**

Exciting Ideas for Organizing Work 95
One More Time – Participation and Empowerment 96
Empowerment 96
Teams, Teams, Teams 100
Self-Managing Teams – Revolution in the Workplace . . . 104
Yes, We Can Make Teams More Effective 108
Summary – Three Key Points 109

Chapter 9   How Can Middle Managers Handle
Work Overload in Daily Operations? 111
Who Are Middle Managers? 112
Review of Causes of Work Overload 112
How Middle Managers Can Use Teams to
    Reduce Work Overload 113
Where Do Middle Managers Spend Their Time? 114
Departmental Planning and Administration 115
Firefighting 119
Personnel Issues 121
Meetings 124
Managing Information 125
Business Travel 127
Who Are Individual Professional Contributors? 128
Overload in the Personal Life of Middle Managers
    and Professional Contributors 130
Care and Well-Being of Middle Managers –
    Lessons From Athletes 131
How Long Does It Take Stress Management to Work? . . 136
Can't We Act on Work Overload Tomorrow? 137
Summary – Three Key Points 138

Chapter 10   What Is the Role of Upper Management
in Work Overload? 139
My Perceptions About Upper Management 139
How to Convince Upper Management That
    Work Overload Is a Serious Problem 141
Find Out the Extent of Work Overload 142
Analysis of the Overload Data 143
Convincing Upper Management to Act on
    Work Overload 145
Issues for Upper Management to Consider
    on Work Overload 147
Developing a Strategy on Work Overload 149

Operational Actions That Upper Management
     Must Take   156
Summary – Three Key Points   158

**Chapter 11 What Are Work and Family Issues
in Work Overload?** **161**
Work and Family Life – Times Have Changed   162
The Pace of Family Life   164
What Organizations Are Doing to Help
     – Seven Activities   165
Elimination of Mandatory Overtime   169
The Top Companies on Work-Family Programs   170
Benefits of Work-Family Programs   170
How to Institute Work-Family Programs   171
Work-Family Programs at the Marriott Corporation . . .   172
Sources of Information on Work-Family Programs   175
Summary – Three Key Points   176

Chapter 12 What Do We Do Next? **177**
A Recap   177
Swing into Action   179
What Should Upper Management Do Next?   179
What Should Middle Management Do Next?   180
A Closing Note   181

**Appendix A Can't We Act Tomorrow on
Work Overload?** **183**

Appendix B List of Actions by Middle Management **185**

Appendix C List of Actions by Upper Management **189**

Appendix D Actions to Minimize Work Overload **191**

Appendix E Stress Reducing Techniques **193**

References *197*

About the Author *203*

Index *205*

List of Figures
and Tables

Figure 1.1	Our working society	2
Table 1.1	Survey results	4
Table 1.2	Work overload – self-assessment	9
Figure 3.1	Work flow in a functional organization	21
Figure 3.2	High-level flow diagram to admit ER patient	27
Figure 3.3	Service blueprint diagram	29
Figure 3.4	Flow diagram with rework loops (identified with triangles)	32
Figure 3.5	Analyzing a flow diagram	33
Figure 4.1	Process guidelines	38
Table 5.1	Mental demands and job content	44
Table 5.2	Mental demands and management practices	48
Table 6.1	Characteristic of jobs	54
Table 6.2	Self-control in the manufacturing sector	62
Table 6.3	Self-control in the service sector	68
Figure 7.1	Attributes for a position	81

Table 7.1   Finding the right people   84

Table 7.2   Job satisfaction factors   90

Table 8.1   Summary of types of teams   101

Table 8.2   Comparison of organizational forms   106

Table 9.1   Ranking by use of Pareto Priority
                 Index (PPI)   117

Figure 9.1   The high performance pyramid   133

Table 10.1   Costs of work overload   142

Table 10.2   Elements to justify action on
                  work overload   145

Table 11.1   10 work family activities   165

Figure 11.1   Proposal-to-plan process   167

Preface

How This Book Can Help You

Often we hear: "Work overload is terrible, but it's a reality of modern life and we really can't do anything about it." Poppycock – and worse. We *can* do something about work overload.

Yes, the pressures are there to cause work overload: the organization must become "lean," jobs have excessive mental demands, globalization, customer expectations, and mergers. Also, our personal lives have changed, for example, two spouses working and a lengthy schedule of sports and other activities for our children and ourselves. These may be exciting times, but they are also busy times. This book addresses the job and family activities that make our lives so busy.

The key result of work overload is the mental and physical stress on individuals and their families. It's not right and we must take action. This book is meant to help those of you who have work overload in both line and staff positions in the manufacturing and service sectors.

We must reduce work overload to make life easier for people in all levels of our working society. This is *not* a book about:

- Teaching people how to handle the stress due to work overload

- Motivating people to love their jobs

- Achieving higher productivity

This book views work overload as a failure of the design of the work. We must analyze the work to identify areas of waste, eliminate the waste, and then use the saved resources to eliminate the work overload and prevent it from happening again. In analyzing the work, we must recognize that overload creates excessive mental demands due to both job content and poor management practices. The book furnishes checklists to help redesign the jobs.

But surely you think that we cannot reduce work overload unless upper and middle management are convinced that the problem is serious enough to act on and also given a plan of what to do. I hear you. This book hits those two issues head on.

A word about the roadmap of the book to help you use the book most effectively: Chapter 1 gives information about the seriousness of the problem (and includes a self-assessment). Chapter 2 summarizes my personal research on work overload. Chapters 3 through 6 cover the analysis of work and the redesign of jobs to reduce overload. Chapter 7 addresses matching work to people and Chapter 8 covers participation and empowerment of people. Chapter 9 describes the issues that middle managers face in addressing work overload. It also provides a summary of stress management concepts. Chapter 10 tackles the toughest problem – upper management. Chapter 11 describes some excellent work and family programs developed by companies. Chapter 12 sums it up and itemizes a few short-range and long-range actions for middle management and for upper management.

I wrote this book to blast the complacency that exists on work overload. As the Canadians would say, let's strike forth.

Acknowledgments

L et me start with the reviewers of the manuscript. They are real professionals. Their efforts – a labor of love under tight deadlines – supplied me with extremely useful comments.

My friends at several organizations helped me to collect survey data on work overload from their part-time graduate students who were working full time in the business world. These people are Aaron Buchko of Bradley University; Lawrence Aft of Aft Systems Inc.; Al Endres of North Central University; and Thomas Browdy, Clifford Schoep, Vincent DeBlaze, and Eugene Mariani of Washington University in St. Louis. A meeting at the AAIM Management Association in St. Louis also furnished some survey data.

My son, Derek, was with me all the way on this manuscript. He kept reviewing the manuscript in all phases and provided spirited examples.

Dean Joseph McCann and Joyce Keller of the University of Tampa helped me with office space and computer assistance during the research phases of this project.

Dr. Edward Chang of Maryville University and my neighbor, Richard Juenger, helped me over the computer problems.

In creating a book, the greatest burden is on the author's family. My wife continues to amaze me with her patience and support. Thanks again, Dee.

1

How Serious Is the Work Overload Issue?

That wonderful book Cheaper by the Dozen *brings to life the true story of Frank and Lillian Gilbreth and their dozen children. Frank and (Dr.) Lillian were industrial engineering pioneers. Industrial engineers study how work is performed and redesign the work to be more efficient and less tiring. The movie (original version 1950) describes – hilariously – how they applied "motion economy" principles to family life. But the Gilbreths also applied the principles to the design of work in the business world. They would turn over in their graves if they saw the frantic pace that many workers lead in today's business world. The Gilbreth idea of efficiency is not the work overload that many people suffer today.*

WHO SUFFERS FROM WORK OVERLOAD?

Nothing is duller than people talking about their overload at work – until someone burns out and resigns. Work overload can occur for any members of our working society (see Figure 1.1):

- Upper management, for example, president, executive vice-president, plant, or site manager

- Managers in the operations functions – the heart of any manufacturing or service organization

- Managers in other functions, for example, product development, purchasing, marketing, and customer service

- Managers of staff departments, for example, human resources, finance, accounting, quality

- Individual professional contributors in all functional areas – the highly educated and skilled people who provide the expertise for our businesses and society

- The hourly workforce, for example, bank tellers, call center operators, operations floor workers, manufacturing workers

This book is aimed at management – upper management and middle management – because only management can take the actions to relieve work overload.

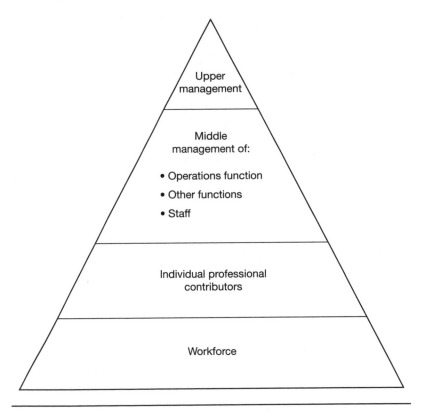

Figure 1.1   Our working society.

THE WARNING SIGNS OF WORK OVERLOAD

Work overload happens when job demands exceed the time and resources available. You know the common symptoms:

- Long workdays, often with the eyes at half mast.

- Unwanted overtime, paid or unpaid.

- State and federal lawsuits accusing companies of avoiding overtime pay by requiring hourly employees to work "off the clock" or reclassifying hourly employees as managerial. Also, suits by managerial and professional employees claim that they must work excessive hours without overtime pay. Overtime can be abusive.

- Inability to meet goals with available time and resources.

- Difficulty in taking vacation time.

- Responding to work problems during nonwork time, including taking work home.

- Frequent "firefighting," usually as unexpected as a sneeze.

- "Add on" tasks making it difficult to focus on the core job.

- Lost work days due to illness.

- Borrowing employees from other activities to fill in for absent employees.

- Frequent interruptions.

- Errors caused by tired employees.

- Add your own to this list.

We can ask our people to give 110 percent occasionally, but not every day. Some people work 24/7 – many managers and professionals are "on call" 24 hours a day, 7 days a week. Those extra hours are usually not recorded and lead to productivity figures that are overstated.

These symptoms snowball when managerial style involves criticism without help, threats, intimidation (both direct and subtle), and bullying. Yes, bullying. Would you believe that the UK National Workplace Bullying Advice Line has a website called "Bully On Line?" But before we go deeper, we must define two terms.

Work overload leads to "stress" – the harmful emotional and physical responses when the requirements of a job do not match the capabilities, resources, or needs of the worker. "Burnout" is the state of physical or emotional exhaustion that results from long-term stress or frustration.

Work overload is only one of many organizational factors that lead to stress. Other factors include role uncertainty and role conflict, responsibility for other people, job dissatisfaction, and job insecurity (more on these factors later). Sometimes, the result is . . . despair. This book transforms despair to hope and satisfaction.

TO WHAT EXTENT IS WORK OVERLOAD COMMON?

The media and the Internet proclaim that work overload is a serious problem. The stories make fascinating reading, but my research reaches this reality: work overload is a serious problem in some companies and jobs; work overload is not a problem in other companies or jobs.

My compliments to those organizations that design jobs and provide sufficient resources to prevent work overload. But many other organizations suffer from work overload, and the problem is particularly serious in industries where customer contact is intensive and continuous and where communication is super fast and essential (for example, call centers, healthcare).

Let's look at some research. The Families and Work Institute (Galinsky, Kim, and Bond 2001) provides us with research of 1003 employees – about two thirds of whom are managers and professional employees and one third other employees. Table 1.1 shows the results.

Table 1.1 Survey results.

- 28 percent of employees felt "overworked" often or very often in the past three months
- 28 percent felt "overwhelmed by how much work they had to do" often or very often in the past three months
- 29 percent felt that they "didn't have the time to step back and process or reflect on the work they're doing" often or very often during the past three months
- 46 percent responded "often" or "very often" to at least one of the previous questions

---

My own research in the manufacturing and service sectors confirms the work overload problem. Of 168 managers and professional employees, 107 (64 percent) responded "yes" when asked if "you experienced work overload, for a continuous period of at least several months."

These numbers express the perceptions (opinions) of people. As my friend, Dean Jeff Klepfer (a psychologist) of The University of Tampa, points out: perceptions are not physical facts, but they are psychological facts. When people feel they have work overload, then stress is threatening.

The International Labor Organization of the United Nations reports that Americans now work more total hours annually (1979) than any other country – nearly a week longer than in 1990. Reich (2001) reports that Americans work 350 hours per year more than Europeans.

We all know of dramatic individual cases of work overload, but serious researchers refer to these cases as "anecdotal evidence" that are not sufficient to draw general conclusions. (As one example, medical residents are people with a medical degree who spend three to seven years training as specialists. Many residents complain that they work 100 or more hours per week. Action has been taken – new rules will limit the workweek to 80 hours. Wow.) Nevertheless, some countries like England and Australia even have an annual national awareness week on work overload.

To keep work overload in perspective, we need to recognize that many people do not have work overload. My friend, Larry Aft, views a large pile of work as simply unfinished worthwhile projects. What a perfect match of a person and a job (more later on matching people and jobs). Some people enjoy their job so much they just work, and work, and work. Some of you will find that appealing; some of you will find that appalling.

We also have extraordinary people who are able to perform miraculously on their jobs (with long hours) but still find the time for their family. Working moms with professional careers are a great example. But such people are not the average. Also, if a wife is not working she carries most of the burden of raising the kids. The husband believes he understands this, but he may be working such long hours that he is *not* aware of the total burden on his wife.

Many people suffering from work overload are highly educated, self-motivated, and attracted to demanding jobs where the risks and rewards are high. Bob Williams is a research scientist in a pharmaceutical manufacturing organization. *He likes his work*, but his workweek is typically 50 hours (with an occasional 60-65 hours per week). This schedule interferes with family activities (he has a wife and two children), and he doesn't like that. Perhaps you are in the same swamp.

       Russian proverb: Don't overwork a willing horse.

Finally, some industries go through extraordinary times requiring long work hours. In the early days of the space program when the United States was racing against the USSR, work overload was a reality, but we rarely heard anyone complain – the excitement and urgency made us feel that we had a job to do and we did it.

But the bottom line is this: many people suffer from work overload.

Is work overload a new problem? Of course not. Then why hasn't the problem been solved before? First, the good scenario. Some middle managers and workforce people tell their superiors about the overload problem once, or even twice. These superiors try to correct the problem, but other important matters prevent them from resolving the overload issue. Managers and workers are aware of this, are sympathetic to the burdens of their bosses, and therefore do not persist but just grunt and groan. Now the bad scenario. Some middle managers (and workforce people) fear that if they complain the boss will conclude that the manager is not able to handle the job and should be replaced. This book addresses such tough issues.

WHAT ARE THE REASONS FOR WORK OVERLOAD?

Prevailing wisdom says that work overload is due to several reasons:

- Competitiveness among companies. We must become "lean" to meet competition – but how lean can we get?

- Globalization. Americans benefit from lower wage rates in foreign countries because we can purchase their goods at lower prices. But this competition puts pressure on American firms to reduce costs and can result in work overload for American workers. Also, as the value of the American dollar in Europe increases, American goods cost more to buy in Europe leading to less demand for American products. This in turn adds pressure to cut costs in America ("run lean"). As we will see later, eliminating the waste in work processes helps us to compete and can prevent work overload.

- Customer expectations. Customers expect faster and faster service, and technology makes that service possible.

- Mergers, acquisitions, and downsizing. This leads to a reduction in jobs and likely work overload for those surviving the job reductions.

- Expansion of family activities. Our relative affluence enables us to enjoy sports and other activities for our children and ourselves. But these activities add to our time commitment.

- The ever-present desire to improve our standard of living. This desire puts economic pressure on the wage earner(s) to earn sufficient salary to meet family needs. We then work longer hours to achieve a promotion or just to provide job security. Moonlighting (two jobs) may be necessary to achieve the needed income level. Data from the Families and Work Institute indicates that 13 percent of Americans are now holding second jobs. DeGraaf,Waan, and Naylor (2002) calls this "affluenza," which they define as "a painful, contagious, socially transmitted condition of overload, debt, anxiety, and waste resulting from the dogged pursuit of more." Rapoport, Bailyn, Fletcher, and Pruitt (2002) suggest an even broader approach to address work-family issues. They propose that work be analyzed to cover a "dual agenda":

  1. The roles of men and women in family, community, and paid work ("gender equity")

  2. How work is done, including wasted time due to inefficient practices

- Everyday living adds to the problem. How about rush-hour traffic, shopping, housework, even holiday trips?

- Add your own to this list.

These forces are mighty strong, but we need to move from these broad issues to the actions needed to relieve work overload. First, what are the consequences of work overload?

HOW DO WE REACT TO WORK OVERLOAD?

Some consequences of work overload are obvious and some are not. We don't need to overstate the case but let's understand what work overload does to people.

Clearly, the key effect is the increase in stress (mental and physical) on individuals and their families.

- This reason alone is certainly enough to act on work overload. But other penalties emerge.

- Work overload reduces job satisfaction and eventually leads to turnover – particularly of key middle managers. Further, when these managers switch to another organization they hire away some of their former colleagues who still suffer from work overload. In a refreshingly frank article, Munck (2001) describes how Marriott found it difficult to recruit and retain talented people because of a deeply ingrained culture of "face time" – the more hours you put in, the better. For a summary of the action taken by Marriott, see Chapter 11.

- Work overload causes errors in products and services. Finding and correcting these errors reduces productivity and increases costs. In addition, overload of front-line employees who deal face to face with customers can result in unpleasant encounters with customers. Also, frustration sets in when employees at all levels observe the poor quality of work.

- Work overload causes errors that can result in injuries to employees and to customers. It's not just an accident on the job, but it's also the accident that occurs when an overworked employee drives home from work. We shudder when we read about injuries and even deaths caused by overworked healthcare workers.

- Add your own to this list.

So where does this lead us? Evaluate your status on work overload.

WORK OVERLOAD – SELF-ASSESSMENT

Rate how often each situation occurs. To record your score, use a scale of 0 to 6 with 0 meaning "almost never" and 6 meaning "almost always." Add up the ratings to get your score.

My workload

1. I am at my company location more than 50 hours per week. _____

2. I take work home and/or receive work-related calls at home. _____

3. Work demands make it difficult for me to schedule vacations. _____

4 I am asked to do additional tasks without being provided with additional resources. _____

5. My department does not have enough resources to handle a normal workload. _____

The job itself

6. My job has a high degree of mental intensity and pressure (for example, internal/external forces, production goals, irate customers, information overload). _____

7. My responsibilities are unclear, and I don't have control of setting priorities, deciding work methods, and use of resources. _____

8. The job content is distasteful (for example, boring, unimportant, underutilizes my skills, poor working conditions). _____

9. The work process provided to me cannot meet the job requirements on quantity and/or quality that I am expected to achieve. _____

10. The feedback provided to me on my performance is inadequate or unfair. _____

11. I am concerned about my career (for example, job security, lack of advancement opportunities, financial compensation). _____

continued

continued

The organization

12. Personnel requisitions in my work area are frequently unfilled for two or more months. _____

13. People resign from our organization because of work overload or other reasons of job dissatisfaction. _____

14. Cooperation among employees is poor. _____

15. The trust and respect among management and employees is poor. _____

16. The organization is insensitive to the demands of work vs. the demands of family. _____

SCORING   WORK OVERLOAD STATUS

0 to 32   Moderate: Take preventive action to keep work overload from getting worse.

33 to 64   Serious: Take steps to substantially reduce work overload within the next few months.

65 to 96   Critical: If work overload cannot be substantially reduced within the next few months, immediately search for another position.

VIEWPOINTS OF THIS BOOK

First, let's go over what this book is not. This book does not teach employees how to handle the stress due to work overload. Also, this is not a book on motivating workers to love their jobs. And, this is not a book on how to achieve higher productivity. Americans are proud of the increase in productivity, but the benefits are offset by our failure to solve the work overload issue.

This book views work overload as a failure of the design of the work activity. The work activity includes resources, work plans, organization of activities, match of job requirements and employee skills, and other factors. We discuss how to redesign the work to eliminate and prevent the work overload.

Work overload often becomes a chronic and inevitable way of life. Chronic work overload requires strong action – on the part of management. This book specifies – in detail – both the short-term and the long-term actions needed by middle management and upper management.

The book cites the names of organizations that take positive action on work overload. This may convince other companies (unnamed, but examples cited) to act.

You probably know of concepts such as simplifying your life, setting a personal vision and goals, and other concepts concerning our lives. These concepts are logical and worthwhile – but for many of us they are difficult to put into practice and do not reflect the realities of the working world.

Action on work overload requires a sense of urgency. We do not have to accept work overload as inevitable. You may call it a "challenge" or call it "an opportunity," but I choose not to sugar coat the issue. Work overload is a problem and we need to take action.

SUMMARY – THREE KEY POINTS

1. Work overload is serious and we must take the initiative to act.

2. People who suffer from work overload are highly educated, self-motivated, and attracted to demanding jobs where the risks and rewards are high. They are the lifeblood of any organization.

3. The pivotal backlash of work overload is the increase in stress (mental and physical) on individuals and their families.

Where to start? How about the causes.

2

What Are the Causes of Work Overload?

> *You know people like Joe. He's a great supervisor in a banking operation for sorting checks. He's a family man, with a wife and three children – always a smile.*
>
> *Checks must be sorted by the end of each day, otherwise, havoc. He has a classical stressful operations job – fire drills, computer breakdowns, absent employees. Joe once worked 14 straight days, 12 hours a day, always on his feet. He made more in overtime pay than base salary. "Joe is the only guy who can handle these problems." Overload still exists, coupled with many mental demands.*

THE 10 CONTRIBUTING CAUSES OF WORK OVERLOAD

My research with operations managers and professional contributors identifies 10 key causes (listed in order of importance):

- Insufficient resources
- Firefighting
- Lack of control of the work process
- Work process not capable
- Unclear goals and responsibilities

- Inputs from suppliers

- Inadequate selection and training

- Information overload

- Computer problems

- Other

The research results come from middle managers and individual professional contributors in the manufacturing and service sectors. They work in four metropolitan areas – Tampa, St. Louis, Atlanta, and Peoria.

The inputs are perceptions of people – with all the usual biases. But perceptions are an important reality because they affect people's feelings and actions. Further, all of these people said they have work overload.

Now let's examine some issues involved in these causes.

1. Insufficient Resources to Handle the Normal Workload.

Some issues involved are:

- What are the short-term and long-term actions to obtain resources to handle the normal workload?

- How much effort could we save by reducing the amount of wasted resources in a process due to errors, corrections, and nonvalue-added steps?

- After we eliminate the waste, how can we convince upper management to use the savings to reduce work overload?

2. Firefighting on Problems.

We need to address issues such as:

- How should we set priorities for firefighting?

- How can we reduce firefighting?

- Who should do the firefighting?

My data show that the first two causes (resources and firefighting) cause about 40 percent of work overload.

3. Lack of Control in Setting Priorities, Deciding Work Methods, and the Use of Resources.

Some issues:

- How should we set priorities?

- How should we decide on work methods?

To what extent should workers participate in planning work methods?

4. The Work Process Is Not Capable of Meeting the Quantity and Quality Requirements.

We need to learn:

- How can we identify the sources of wasted effort in a process?

- How can we determine if the process is capable?

- If the process is not capable, where will the resources come from to redesign the work process to make it capable?

From my research data, these first four causes (resources, fire-fighting, lack of control, and work process not capable) cause about 60 percent of the overload problem.

5. Unclear Performance Goals and Responsibilities.

Let's investigate:

- On what parameters are performance goals needed?

- Do we need to set a goal to limit work overload?

- How can we translate the vague subject of "responsibility" into specific actions and reach agreement on who should take which actions?

6. Inputs from Internal/External Suppliers – Missing, Wrong, Late.

Some issues:

- What actions can we take to prevent problems with internal suppliers?

- What actions can we take to prevent problems with external suppliers?

- How can upper management help on problems with external suppliers?

7. Inadequate Selection and Training of Personnel.

Key questions are:

- How can we match job requirements to employee skills?

- What special approaches can we take to recruit new personnel, particularly at low salary levels?

- Has the adequacy of the training been verified?

- When positions cannot be filled, what actions can we take to minimize work overload on other employees?

8. Information Overload – E-mail and Other.

Some issues are:

- How should we set priorities to respond to information arriving in our workplace ("pushed information")? This includes e-mails, letters, memos, telephone calls, journals, and the like.

- How can we best acquire and use retrievable ("pulled") information. This information resides on the web, in online journals, in discussions with colleagues, and other sources.

- How can the priority nightmare of e-mails be handled – who sent the e-mail, the subject, or other criteria?

9. Computer Hardware or Software Problems.

Some questions:

- How can we identify chronic computer hardware problems and present information to information technology (IT) management that will assure action?

- How can we identify chronic computer software problems and present information to IT management that will assure action?

- How does computer system downtime contribute to work overload?

10. Other Problems Causing Work Overload.

Some issues involved are:

- How can we address changing priorities and strategies in an organization to minimize work overload?

- What is the relation between insufficient resources to meet job requirements and the mental demands required in jobs?

- How can we discover the reasons for work overload that are unique to our organization?

We will discuss all of the issues. Note, however, that the causes have a common element – deficiencies in the work processes. Thus, we will focus on studying the work processes to reduce work overload.

IS WORK OVERLOAD A HEAVY HITTER TO JOB SATISFACTION?

Yes. Specifically, work overload is one of several factors that have an impact on job satisfaction. We will examine these job satisfaction factors in Chapter 7. But this book is about work overload, and we will focus on that subject rather than discuss job satisfaction and get lost in a jungle.

Let's hope that work overload is a small problem in your organization, but . . .

◁ *Old Russian proverb: A small hole can sink a big ship.* ▷

SUMMARY – THREE KEY POINTS

Those with work overload perceive that the top three causes are:

1. Insufficient resources to handle the normal workload

2. Firefighting on problems

3. Lack of control in setting priorities, deciding work methods, and use of resources

Would you agree with these for your company?

All causes of work overload emerge from the work itself, and so we will next move on to studying work as a process.

3

Why Study Waste in a Process?

An operation at a manufacturing organization requires three shifts. At the beginning of a shift, a brief review of work status takes place. The key question is this: "Do we have enough people for this shift – how many are here?" Absentees are a problem and often the supervisor must do the work of an absentee. Near the end of a shift, all in the work crew watch to see how many will show up for the next shift; if the next shift has absentees then the supervisor asks one or two people to stay on for the next shift. All of this on a moment's notice. What a stressful situation – in addition to the work overload. Why not hire more people (but there is no money in the budget); cross train people and borrow them from other areas when necessary (but that creates problems of work overload for the areas from whom employees are borrowed). So we now have work overload.

DO WE CHANGE THE WORK OR CHANGE THE PERSON?

We can learn more about the reasons for work overload by studying the work itself. Overload means primarily a failure of the design of the work system, not a failure of the people doing the work. To correct current work overload – and to prevent future work overload – we must change the work design or add resources rather than teach employees how to handle the stress due to overload. Stress reduction concepts are a valuable supplement (see Chapter 9 for some suggestions), but those concepts focus on the effect rather than the cause. This book focuses on the design of the work. We start with the concept of the work process.

ALL WORK IS DONE IN A PROCESS

A process is a collection of activities (individual jobs) that converts inputs into outputs or results. A simple process has several individual jobs; a complex process has many individual jobs. Examples from manufacturing are producing a printed circuit board or creating loaves of bread. Examples from service might be making customer reservations at a hotel call center or admitting a patient at a hospital.

Experience suggests that achieving business goals depends mostly on large, complex processes that go across functional departments. Examples of such cross-functional processes are product development, billing, assembly, hospital patient care, and insurance claims servicing.

A *primary* process is a collection of cross-functional activities essential for external customer satisfaction and for achieving the mission of the organization. These activities integrate people, materials, work methods, energy, equipment, and information. The managers of functional departments are responsible for functional pieces of the process, but often no one is accountable for the entire cross-functional process. Problems arise because managers focus on meeting functional objectives rather than process objectives (see Figure 3.1).

Modern process management techniques include measurements to serve as drivers to help achieve process objectives (see Gryna 2001, Chapter 6).

We will first study work at the process level before studying the work within individual jobs. For many processes, 30 percent of the work performed is waste – waste that saps human resources and leads to work overload. Yes, the number is surprising, but it is based on my experience with processes that have not been analyzed for the many forms of waste. Chapter 2 reports the number one culprit of work overload as insufficient resources to handle a normal workload. If we can identify and eliminate the waste in a process then resources become available to reduce the work overload. This chapter analyzes work at the process level and identifies the waste; Chapter 6 analyzes work at the individual job level.

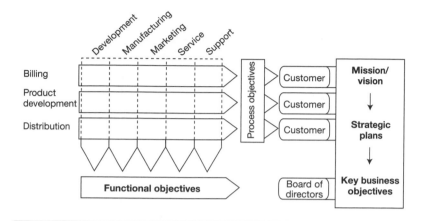

Figure 3.1 Work flow in a functional organization.
Source: Juran Institute, Wilton, CT, www.Juran.com. Used with permission.

WHAT ARE THE FORMS OF WASTE IN A PROCESS?

Waste takes several forms:

- **Firefighting.** Every organization does firefighting, that is, reacting to unexpected problems that arise during day-to-day (or even hour-to-hour) business. The range of problems is endless, for example, computer breakdowns, missing or wrong inputs from internal or external suppliers, absent employees, and so on. In theory, if we do a better job of planning or anticipating our activities then we can prevent firefighting. In practice, that simply doesn't happen. At best, we can reduce firefighting. My research indicates that firefighting is a significant contributor to work overload.

  Action: In Chapter 9, we discuss some approaches to reducing firefighting. If we reduce firefighting, then we free up resources to reduce work overload.

- **Rework to correct errors.** Rework means doing the job twice because it wasn't done right the first time. The rework may be partial to correct a deficiency or may be complete because the product or service had to be discarded. Let's face it – some errors will always occur, but many processes run 10 percent or more rework. Even a small percent of rework has an enormous impact when applied to a large volume of activity, for example, 0.7 percent of packages delivered to the wrong city by a major delivery service means 10,000 packages per week or more than a half million packages annually.

Action: Diagnose the process to determine the process stability and the causes of the rework. Then remove the causes, and use the resources saved to reduce work overload.

- **Steps of marginal importance to a customer** (the buzz word is "nonvalue-added"). At Marriott, managers reported that they were spending about 11.7 hours per week on low-value work. After a Management Flexibility pilot program, the time spent on low-value work had been reduced to 6.8 hours per week.

  Action: If you cannot justify these steps, then eliminate the steps and thus reduce work overload.

- **Unnecessary steps in a process.** The process is initially designed with steps to meet customer needs. Perhaps the original reason for some of these steps has disappeared but the steps remain in the process. A good question to ask is: "What would happen if this step was eliminated?"

  Action: Amputate these steps and use the resources saved to reduce work overload.

- **Excessive inspection to find errors.** Inspection is a vital part of business activities. Human beings are not perfect and so we need inspection to give assurance that the customer receives good product. But when the level of errors in a process is high, then the level of inspection must be high to catch all (maybe) the errors. Such processes must be changed to reduce the errors.

  Although the term inspection usually refers to manufacturing industries, the term also applies to service industries. In the service sector, inspection is called review, checking, reconciliation, or examination. The evaluation of an income tax return, the cleanliness of a hotel room, or the accuracy of a bank teller's closing balance are really all forms of inspection – a measurement, a comparison to a standard, and a decision. We should not eliminate inspection or other forms of review, but we may be able to reduce the frequency.

Action: After we determine and *eliminate* the causes of errors, then we can reduce the inspection and use the resources to relieve work overload.

This book explains how to analyze processes for waste, but first, let's address two questions that you are burning to ask: 1) who is going to do these analyses? and 2) even if we eliminate the waste how can we be sure that the savings in resources help to reduce work overload rather than be taken as cost savings, that is, sent to the bottom line?

WHO WILL DO THE ANALYSES TO ELIMINATE PROCESS WASTE?

Let's set the record straight. You – the operations manager or the professional specialist – won't do these analyses because you're overloaded with work. I won't try to convince you to find time. And it's not just the time that's needed but also the basic skills to do the analyses. So who can do it?

- An industrial engineering (IE) department – if you have one (and you should). The names vary, that is, industrial engineering, operations engineering, performance improvement, management services. The IE's (including Frank and Lillian Gilbreth) are the pioneers in work simplification and have the skills to analyze the processes. Put them to work for you as your internal consultant. You should select the process or processes and tell the IEs that you want them to reduce work overload, not to reduce costs.

- A quality department – if you have one (and you should). The names vary, that is, quality, quality assurance, quality management, Six Sigma, performance management. Quality professionals make major contributions to process analysis and can help you. Again, select the process and have them focus the analysis on reducing work overload.

- Any other staff department that has the skills and that could be enlisted to help you. One possibility is the human resources department – if you still have one (and you should). Another possibility is the audit group in a finance department. Some companies like Baxter Healthcare and

Exxon Mobil broaden their financial audit function to include a focus on improvement of work processes.

- A cross-functional team consisting of senior personnel or managers from the various departments having activities in the process. Such people know the process better than anyone else in the organization. Two obstacles may arise: 1) in a situation of work overload, these people do not have the time to study the process; and 2) they probably do not have the skills needed to study work at the process level. They certainly could be taught the skills needed but again time will be required. If time could somehow be made available then a cross-functional team would be the first choice to study the process. Judith Lyons of Vista Plan Solution has a practical suggestion to encourage such a team. Promise them up front that their role is to study and redesign the process, but they will not have to revise the procedures and other documentation about the process. Staff people will handle the paperwork revision. People in operating functions are anxious to participate in improving a process, but they hate to spend time revising the procedures.

- An external consultant. This requires approval by upper management (see Chapter 10).

- A local college. First, find out who are the professors active with the business world. They want their students to get "real-world" experience. Ask them if they have a team of students who would like to gain experience analyzing a process in your department. The students will not solve your work overload problem, but they can at least document the process in a flow diagram (explained next). With this much analysis done, you could finish the analysis and find ways to reduce the work overload.

Bradley University has 35 years experience with a required senior industrial engineering course in which student teams (under the direction of one or more professors) take a vaguely defined problem (like "work overload in this department"), analyze the process(es), and recommend and present recommendations for solving and implementing the solution. Trust me, this works. If you decide to contact a college, the appropriate departments for you to contact are industrial engineering, industrial technology, or operations management.

Whoever does the process analysis should make sure he or she involves the people doing the jobs by asking their opinions about the process. Don't expect them to do the analysis – they don't have the time (work overload) or the skills. But they know the jobs better than anyone else and those jobs affect their careers. You must convince them that the analysis will help them (not eliminate their jobs). Why not guarantee that no one will lose a job or take a decreased salary?

Once it is known who will do the analysis, then we are ready to proceed. Obtain authorization from upper management to analyze one process as an experiment. Much rides on this experiment, that is, a successful case will jump start additional projects to discover and eliminate process waste.

Use some of the savings from process analyses to provide resources for analyses on additional processes. Sometimes this can be a win/win situation. At Caterpillar Tractor Co., several improvement projects resulted in reducing the amount of inspection of certain products. Some inspectors became available for other work. Caterpillar trained them to do process analysis, changed their position and salary, and thus provided the resources for further process analysis work.

HOW CAN WE BE SURE THAT SAVINGS IN PROCESS WASTE WILL BE USED TO PROVIDE RESOURCES TO REDUCE WORK OVERLOAD?

We can't be sure. But, before we analyze processes, we can ask upper management to commit that any savings in time and resources apply to reducing work overload.

Even if we eliminate waste from processes, middle management may still have work overload in managing departments. We will address that matter in Chapter 9, Running Daily Operations.

We are ready now to discuss how to analyze for waste in a process.

ANALYZING FOR WASTE IN A PROCESS

The main steps are: define the boundaries of the process, identify the customers, discover customer needs, prepare a flow diagram for the process, establish process measurements, analyze process data, and redesign the process. We will discuss these steps next, but for a more complete coverage see Gryna 2001.

Define the Boundaries of the Process

This means define the current (or "as is") process in terms of where the process starts, which activities to include (and exclude), and where the process ends. A high-level flow diagram (also called a process map or a value stream map) is a useful tool in this step. A brief process mission statement is also useful.

This diagram shows the scope and major steps in the process. An example is shown in Figure 3.2.

Identify the Customers of the Process

A customer is anyone who is affected by the input or output of the product or process. Three categories of customers then emerge:

1. External customers, both current and potential. External customers (or "stakeholders") include ultimate users but also intermediate processors as well as merchants. Other "customers" are not purchasers but have some connection with the product, for example, government regulatory bodies, shareholders, partners, investors, the media, and the public. External customers clearly are of primary importance.

2. Internal customers. When the purchasing department receives a specification from engineering for a procurement, purchasing is an internal customer of engineering; when the procurement is executed, then engineering is the internal customer of purchasing. Similarly, at an insurance company, the payroll department and the service department are internal customers of each other.

3. Suppliers as customers. We should view suppliers as internal customer departments just like our internal manufacturing department.

In practice, some customers are more important than others. It is typical that about 75 percent of the sales volume comes from about 20 percent of the customers. These are the "vital few" customers who command priority.

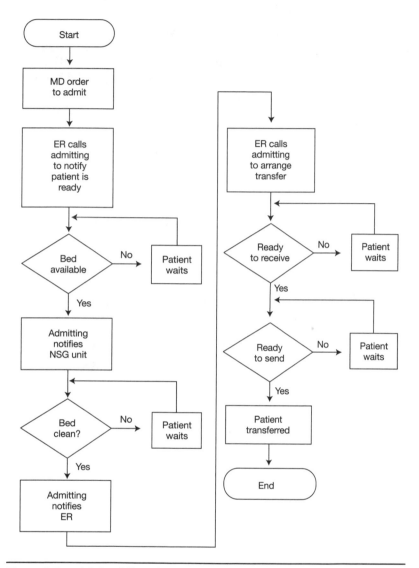

Figure 3.2   High-level flow diagram to admit ER patient.
Source: Juran Institute, Wilton, CT, www.Juran.com. Used with permission.

External customers are the backbone of a company, but they are not all equal in importance. External customers of marginal importance can drain company resources and contribute to work overload. A difficult but important decision involves which current customers to drop and which potential customers not to pursue. A similar decision involves which products to drop. Upper management makes decisions on customer and product composition (see Chapter 10 under Operational Actions That Upper Management Must Take). Reducing the customer base and/or product offerings can not only relieve work overload but also can enable an organization to concentrate resources on the vital few customers and vital few products with activities that lead to customer loyalty. Having identified our customers, we next need to discover customer needs.

Discover Customer Needs

We ask customers directly what their needs are and the relative priorities of those needs. But we also methodically study how customers presently use the product and analyze their total system of use in order to identify hidden needs. This provides ideas to perform surgery on current products and helps to discover needs for new products. Needs are always in flux because today's new needs become a routine expectation tomorrow. Make sure you update customer needs for both external and internal customers. Also, survey the needs of noncustomers, because meeting their needs may increase sales. With respect to work overload, the study of customer needs identifies work activities that contribute little or nothing to customer needs and thus deserve no resources.

Prepare a Flow Diagram of the Process

We next prepare a more detailed flow diagram showing the activities, key customers, suppliers, and their roles in the process. This tells us how the process works.

Schedule a work session of several hours for a team to discuss the process and prepare the flowchart (some people call this value stream mapping). These discussions will reveal disagreements on how the process really works: "No, I don't send that document to accounting." Or, "When you send me the sales order there is always data missing and I must call you for the missing data." Or, "I didn't know what you did with the information I send to you each day."

A facilitator describes how the work session will proceed, asks for inputs on the sequence of activities, and uses devices such as sticky notes to physically create the flowchart on a large board prepared for the purpose. The result is a starting point for analysis and improvement.

Figure 3.3 shows a flow diagram for handling a request for adjustments to customer bills.

This particular flow diagram has some clever additions to the basic diagram. You do not need to include these additions but they

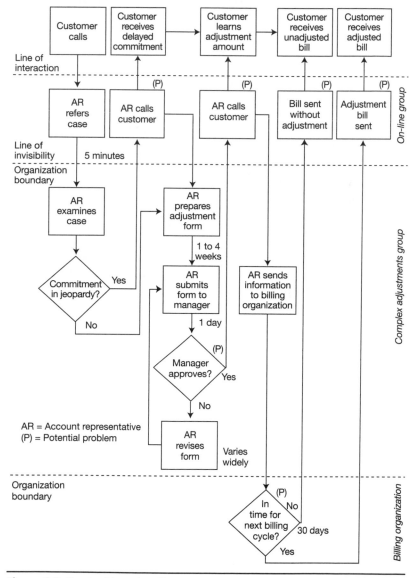

Figure 3.3 Service blueprint diagram.
Source: © 1990 AT&T., all rights reserved. Used with permission.

may be useful to you. The "line of interaction" is the boundary of activities where the customer and frontline employees ("on-line group") have discussions. The "line of invisibility" separates activities that are seen or not seen by customers. The "organization boundary" shows which activities occur in the three departments involved in the process (the on-line group, the complex adjustments group, and the billing organization). This example also illustrates both frontline direct customer contact and back-room or back-office operations. The time required is also shown for some activities. The symbol "P" denotes process points at which problems could occur that would cause customer dissatisfaction and subsequent work overload to correct the dissatisfaction. To prevent problems, we must identify potential problems, usually based on past data or an analysis of the flow diagram.

Establish Process Measurements

Measurements on the output from a process tell us how well the process is doing and set the stage for process analysis and improvement. Also, measurements at intermediate steps in the process help to control process performance and determine the capability of the process to meet quantity and quality requirements. (The process must be stable in order to measure the true process capability). A process that is not capable is the culprit leading to work overload. In deciding what measurements to collect from a process, the emphasis should be on the process mission, quantitative goals, and customer needs discussed previously.

To address work overload, we need to collect data about the overload: at what process steps, how frequently, and the likely causes.

Collecting data on the work overload is an important step to correcting the overload.

Analyze Process Data

In this step, we evaluate the process performance data, identify opportunities for improvement, and determine the causes of process problems (sometimes called "disconnects"). When these problems happen, the people running the process must spend unplanned time to correct the deficiencies, and you know what the result is – work overload.

> *Old Spanish proverb: He who stumbles over the same stone deserves to break his neck*

Causes of process problems span a wide range:

- Inputs from external suppliers
- Inputs from internal suppliers
- Sporadic or chronic computer hardware breakdowns
- Software problems
- Machinery or equipment failures
- Absent employees
- Poorly trained employees
- Other causes

In short, we have a process that simply is not capable of meeting quantity and quality requirements with the current process design and resources assigned.

The high-level and detailed flow diagrams are key tools at this point. For example, at a telecommunications company a team required four hours to construct a high-level flow diagram for a new customer service. The time consumed was a classic case of each member having a different view of how the process operated. The discussion and resulting high-level diagram exposed missing links, bottlenecks, unnecessary steps, and redundancies in the process. For the first time, all team members had a common understanding of the process.

The team then divided the high-level diagram into four segments and constructed detailed flow diagrams for each segment. A portion of one of these is shown in Figure 3.4 (Juran Institute 1989).

Examination of the four detailed flow diagrams revealed 30 rework loops – two of the rework loops (no. 26 and no. 27) are shown with a triangle symbol. But then data showed a surprise, that is, the time spent in six of the 30 loops accounted for 82 percent of the total rework time. Clearly, that's where the effort to reduce rework must concentrate. This revelation illustrates a basic concept of great importance. As applied to work overload: a few contributing causes to work overload are responsible for the bulk of the work overload. This is called the Pareto concept.

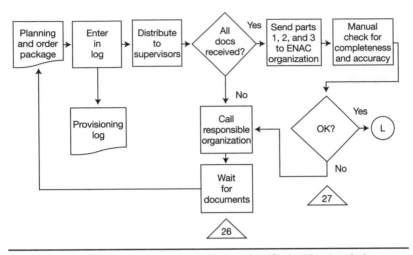

Figure 3.4 Flow diagram with rework loops (identified with triangles).
Source: Juran Institute, Wilton, CT, www.Juran.com. Used with permission.

We must identify these vital few contributors and concentrate our effort to reduce work overload on those contributors. We will apply this concept again later in the book.

Flow diagrams often use four symbols for events: a diamond for a decision-making event, a small square for an activity, a triangle for a rework loop of several activities, and a paper symbol for a document or data base. Figure 3.5 provides a checklist of questions to ask for each of these symbols to help discover opportunities for improvement.

Historically, we owe a debt to the industrial engineering profession for the construction and analysis of flow diagrams along with other simple and complex process analysis techniques. A concise and practical reference on flow diagrams and process maps is *The Basics of Process Mapping* by Robert Damelio (1996).

At the end of the analyze phase, we have a clear understanding of the current process, including waste and other problems and their causes, and we probably have initial thoughts on redesigning the process.

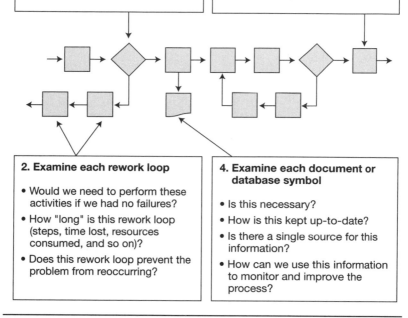

1. Examine each decision symbol

- Is this a checking activity?
- Is this a complete check, or do some types of errors go undetected?
- Is this a redundant check?

3. Examine each activity symbol

- Is this a redundant activity?
- What is the value of this activity relative to its cost?
- How have we prevented errors in this activity?

2. Examine each rework loop

- Would we need to perform these activities if we had no failures?
- How "long" is this rework loop (steps, time lost, resources consumed, and so on)?
- Does this rework loop prevent the problem from reoccurring?

4. Examine each document or database symbol

- Is this necessary?
- How is this kept up-to-date?
- Is there a single source for this information?
- How can we use this information to monitor and improve the process?

Figure 3.5 Analyzing a flow diagram.
Source: Juran Institute, Wilton, CT, www.Juran.com. Used with permission.

REALITY – STAFF LOW, ADD PEOPLE BUT NEVER ENOUGH

Yes, processes have plenty of waste that cause work overload. But another dimension of work overload relates to management practices.

As one manager said to me: many companies staff for the low part of the demand cycle and, as demand grows, they add overtime or people. But they never add enough people (or add untrained people) – they don't want to worry about staffing when demand drops. If necessary – and this is the shocker – they overload their "stars" with extra work. Message to management: it's not fair.

SUMMARY – THREE KEY POINTS

1. To address work overload, redesign the work rather than teach people how to handle the stress of work overload.

2. Work takes place in individual jobs that are grouped together into processes. We should first study work at the process level and then at the job level. Take a broad look first (process) before jumping into details (jobs).

3. Most work processes have significant waste that we can identify and eliminate leading to a reduction in work overload. The waste is there and you can find it.

I end this chapter on a humorous note. An e-mail came across my screen reminding us that people are sometimes asked to give more than 100 percent on the job. Now try some math. Represent the 26 letters of the alphabet as numbers for example, A is 1 percent . . . E is 5 percent . . .T is 20 percent . . . Z is 26 percent. Now convert the letters in "WORK OVERLOAD" to numbers (for example, W is 23 percent). If you add up these numbers, the result is . . . 159 percent.

If we now understand the process causing overload, we can next proceed to redesign the process and relieve the overload.

4

How Can We Redesign Work at the Process Level to Eliminate Work Overload?

It's 2001. Another merger just announced. Two financial institutions. Must convert mainframes. Here we go again.

We need to test the conversion in a production environment and the best time to do the test is 4:00 a.m. to 6:30 a.m. A capacity test is made to make sure that the system can handle the volume of transactions and the number of different users. All three shifts of personnel are present at the same time during the test to handle the test and help load up to full capacity.

We try for five days, but the system test still won't work. Many people sit around doing nothing, waiting for the experts to solve the problem. We even give people gift certificates and extra time off to compensate for the long hours. Morale is devastated – "I'm tired."

PROCESS WASTE AND WORK OVERLOAD

Wasted effort in a process is a main cause of work overload. Chapter 3 provides tools to identify specific forms of waste in processes; this chapter furnishes a roadmap to redesign a process to eliminate the waste and thereby reduce work overload.

Design changes may involve work content, workflow, processing of information, new equipment, and workplace layout – to name just a few areas. Work redesign may also involve making changes in policies and procedures. We can document and review these changes using a revised flow diagram – the "as is" diagram of the current process becomes a "should" diagram of the revised process.

This chapter considers redesign at the process level; Chapters 5 and 6 tackle redesign at the individual job level within the processes.

REDESIGN AT THE PROCESS LEVEL – RADICAL AND INCREMENTAL CHANGE

Redesign (at the process level or the job level) may involve radical change, incremental change, or both. First, let's look at radical change.

The Ford Motor Company provides a classic example of radical change in a process – in this case, the accounts payable process. The accounts payable department employed more than 500 people to make payments to Ford suppliers. These people match: 1) the purchase order sent to suppliers by Ford, 2) the receiving document generated at Ford when the parts were received, and 3) the invoice received by Ford from the supplier. When these three documents match then a clerk issues payment to the supplier. But sometimes the documents don't match – the supplier sent the wrong parts or wrong quantity, the supplier invoice was incorrect, and many, many other reasons. Resolving these cases requires time and exhausting discussions between Ford and the supplier, that is, work overload. Ford was planning to automate some of these detailed functions.

But first, Ford tried benchmarking with a Japanese partner company (Mazda) and learned that Mazda employed not 500 people but five (not 500, not 50, yes five) to handle this accounts payable activity. Mazda is smaller than Ford but the ratio of 500 to five – wow. Ford decided that automating the current activities was not sufficient. Instead, they decided that the scope (boundaries) was not just the activities in the accounts payable department, but instead should cover the entire procurement process, which involved not only accounts payable activities but also a number of steps in different departments at Ford (that is, this is a cross-functional process).

Ford discussions with Mazda about the process (more benchmarking) revealed a radical concept at Mazda.

Mazda did not use an invoice at all. This led to a radical redesign of the process at Ford. Hammer and Champy (1993) provide the details.

Radical redesign of a process (sometimes called reengineering) can achieve great improvements in performance of a process, including the reduction of work overload. But for cross-functional processes the middle managers involved must lead the way.

General Electric and other companies report success with "work out sessions" to achieve process improvements. These sessions last several days and involve front-line personnel and senior management people. A trained facilitator (see Chapter 7) provides assistance at the session. The sessions identify improvement areas, develop action plans, and obtain senior-level approval for action during the session. See also the concept of a "blitz team" in Chapter 8.

Next, we consider an example of an incremental improvement of a process that results in less work overload. This classic example comes from a division of IBM and involves the monthly closing of the financial accounts.

Every monthly closing of the books meant the processing of two million accounting entries. Even though the incoming data was 97.5 percent accurate, 4000 to 6000 miscodes emerged each day during the closing period resulting in high overtime and low morale (work overload). A process analysis yielded significant improvements, including provisions for feedback and stronger requirements for the supplier group. The result was a five-fold improvement in miscodes – and overtime for error code correction was mostly eliminated (see *Fortune* 1985).

An example of a powerful (but more complex) technique is computer simulation of a process. Here, a computer systems model is developed based on the logical sequence of process activities along with data on the activities. The computer model then generates simulated results of process outputs. The time spent in developing the computer model is an investment to help reveal bottlenecks, underutilized process activities, key causes of problems, and to understand the process. Later, the model can also help to evaluate potential solutions to problems. Batson and Williams (1998) describe seven cases, from both manufacturing and service industries, of using simulation in process improvement. You would not have the time to create a computer simulation, but you could ask a staff department to make the simulation model.

Another technique for discovering ideas for process design or redesign involves contacting other organizations having similar processes. Some processes are common across many types of manufacturing and service industries (for example, the hiring process, the accounts payable process as in the Ford/Mazda example) and the experience of these organizations can provide ideas already tested in practice. This is an application of benchmarking, that is, ask other organizations how they carry out their process and why their process works in their environment. If you can obtain a copy of their process flow diagram, so much the better.

To encourage and guide you to make process improvements we next present guidelines on redesign of processes.

GUIDELINES FOR REDESIGN OF PROCESSES

Eliminating waste in a process leads to increased productivity, and we will use the increase in productivity to reduce work overload, including the reduction of mandatory overtime.

These guidelines concern the redesign at the process level. (Chapter 6 presents guidelines for redesign at the job level). Figure 4.1 summarizes the 15 guidelines into five categories.

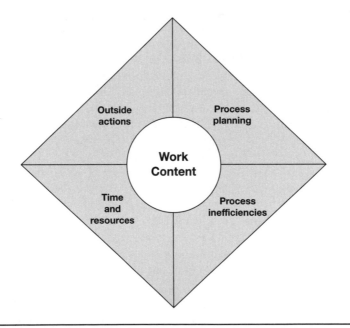

Figure 4.1   Process guidelines.

Work Content

- Use the flow diagram of the process to identify nonvalue-added steps, that is, waste. Some people call this diagram a value stream map. Each step in a process must add value for customers, otherwise eliminate the step. Unclear and illogical steps are often nonvalue-added. Use the forms of waste in Chapter 3 and Figure 3.5 for analyzing a flow diagram.

- Business history is replete with examples of activities originally established to meet an important need. But when the need disappears, or has a lower priority, the activity just continues on and on because no one asks if it adds sufficient value to justify the time and resources spent.

  ✂ *Old Russian proverb: Habit is a shirt that we* ✂
  wear until we die.

- Combine several individual jobs to reduce the repetitive sequence that leads to boredom. This also broadens the skills of individuals and leads to more job satisfaction.

- As an extension of combining narrow jobs, have the individual worker create the entire product or service for the customer. Hewlett-Packard sometimes uses "work stations" (instead of assembly lines) in which an individual worker builds the entire product. This approaches the days of the craftsman rather than the assembly-line worker who performs one narrow job in a sequence of narrow jobs. In the service sector, establish a single point of contact for customers so that one employee handles an entire service, rather than transfer the customer to other employees. Again, this broader scope results in more job satisfaction and perhaps a higher salary.

- Apply state-of-the-art information technology. Sometimes, technology can relieve humans of unpleasant or tedious tasks. Remember how customers in a department store had to wait for a clerk to obtain approval from a supervisor of a customer check. Technology has essentially eliminated that step. Applying the technology often involves two steps: 1) developing the software to perform a certain activity, and 2) teaching the user how to use the software in the job. Ironically, sometimes the software is already available – and even sitting in the computer on an employee's desk. Thus, an employee may have Microsoft Office™ software in the computer but not realize all of the capabilities of that software – let alone know how to use those capabilities. This technology is forever changing. Many companies and colleges offer excellent classes and workshops on new software, for example, Accenture holds an in-house training session every few months explaining how to use the capabilities of the software.

Process Planning

- Focus on the needs of internal and external customers of the process and find out the relative priority of these different needs. Each step in a process must add value for customers, otherwise eliminate the step. Customer needs and priorities will change so keep up to date.

- Make sure that process goals (they should exist) are linked to customer and organization requirements and that these process goals are translated into job goals.

- Watch the "white space" among departments. This is where information and material is transferred across departments. These "handoffs" are often a source of problems because each department focuses on its own goals, often at the urging of senior management. Handoffs, of course, also occur between individuals within one department. The idea is to minimize handoffs.

Process Inefficiencies

- Collect data (or other input from supervisors) to identify any bottleneck steps in a process that cause poor performance and work overload. Would adding resources temporarily eliminate the backlog or is additional action necessary?

- Remove causes of errors in processes to reduce rework and minimize checking and controls. Make sure you collect data to identify the "vital few" errors that are causing most of the total problem in the process (the Pareto rule). Eliminating the vital few errors will not completely solve the problem, but it will eliminate a good chunk of the work overload.

Time and Resources

- Identify overworked personnel (from overtime records, inputs from supervisors, or other means) and study their jobs for relief from work overload.

- If a step must be added to a process, make sure that the step adds value, and that time and resources are available. If not, eliminate some steps from the current process to provide the time. If that isn't possible, then don't add the new step. Make it a test case against work overload.

- In making time estimates for activities do not assume that procedures will be followed exactly. This ideal case never occurs. Add 20 percent to any carefully prepared time estimate to allow for the unexpected, and thereby minimize or prevent work overload.

- Allow sufficient time for "knowledge processes" that involve acquiring, monitoring, processing, and analyzing complex information. Often changing business environments and technologies and their many complex interactions accompany this knowledge. Adding up the times to perform individual steps in knowledge processes is not sufficient. We must add time to synthesize and integrate that information. Some people call this time "slack." Nohria and Gulati (1996) define slack as "the pool of resources in an organization that is in excess of the minimum necessary to produce a given level of organizational output."

- Slack resources may seem inefficient in the short term, but slack is essential for long-term effectiveness and survival. For further discussion, see Lawson (2001) and DeMarco (2001).

Outside Actions

- Consider transferring some activities to suppliers or even to customers.

- Find out how other organizations perform the activity (benchmark).

SUMMARY – THREE KEY POINTS

1. Redesign of work at the process level starts with a focus on the needs of external and internal customers of a process.

2. Redesign may involve work content, workflow, processing of information, new technology, workplace layout, or outside actions.

3. Specific guidelines can help you to redesign a process and smash the work overload.

The next two chapters address how the mental demands of many jobs contribute to work overload and how we can reduce these mental demands through work redesign at the individual job level.

5

How Do the Mental Demands of Work Contribute to Work Overload?

The plot at a bank: Three shifts in four cities must process Monday's checks and finish by 2:00 a.m. A directive from upper management schedules a conference call (minimum of two hours) every Tuesday at 1:00 a.m. to discuss the question: "Will we get all of the Monday checks processed by 2:00 a.m.?"

The call involves 12 middle managers: the site manager (first shift) at each city and two each from other shifts at the four different cities. They discuss the status of production. But much time is spent waiting for the latest status information, so there is plenty of time for the first shift people – half asleep – to talk about their kids, what they're watching on television, and other personal matters. Yes, one of them did fall asleep – they heard him snoring.

When production is not up to par, the epidemic of reasons emerges: people are absent from work, computer system breakdowns, weather problems (the plane flying checks in for processing was delayed) and so on.

Climax: the conference call ends about 3:00 a.m., the first shift managers can now go back to bed – and be at their desks at 7:30 a.m.

LONG HOURS + EXCESSIVE MENTAL DEMANDS = WORK OVERLOAD

The primary culprit in work overload is the lack of time and resources to meet job goals. In Chapters 2 and 3, we considered the contributors to work overload and how to identify the waste in processes that leads to work overload. But another dimension adds to the work overload problem. That dimension is the mental demands of many jobs. Many jobs do not involve excessive mental demands. But add excessive mental demands to insufficient resources and the result can be serious work overload, stress, and even burnout.

When the mental demands become excessive, then frustration sets in. Dean Jeffrey Klepfer of The University of Tampa regards such frustration as a form of waste because it reduces the capacity of a person to handle job demands and results in reaching the work overload state faster. Research (for example, Karasek and Theorell 1990) performed by psychologists, industrial sociologists, and industrial engineers suggests that mental demands on jobs are caused by: 1) job content and 2) poor management practices. This chapter discusses these two elements of mental demands. In the next chapter, we learn how to redesign individual jobs to minimize the impact of mental demands on work overload.

MENTAL DEMANDS AND JOB CONTENT

The mental demand issues and job content are shown in Table 5.1.

Table 5.1 Mental demands and job content.

Mental intensity of the job
- Internal and external forces
- Meeting productivity goals
- Frequent interruptions
- Irate customers
- Firefighting
- Information overload

Time spent on the job
- Total hours

---

continued

continued

• Schedule of hours
• Overtime
• Accessibility during nonwork time
Job content
• Boring jobs
• Underutilizing employee skills
• Meaningfulness of job
• Physical exertion
• Working conditions
Control in doing the job
• Setting priorities
• Deciding work methods
• Use of resources
Social interaction on the job
• Social environment
• Cooperation among employees

MENTAL DEMANDS CAUSED BY JOB CONTENT

Mental Intensity of the Job

Intensity of job content is the tension that results from forces, internal or external to the organization, associated with the nature of the work.

A classic example is pressure to meet productivity goals when management does not allot sufficient time and resources. Management may believe that sufficient time has been allotted but that simply may not be true. Working on too many tasks at the same time is a frequent complaint, as is frequent interruptions. Another example is the flashing of a sign at a call center stating how many calls are waiting to be answered. A further example is dealing with irate customers in person or over the telephone. Some of these customers are correct in being irate; some of them are not. Some of these customers are reasonable; some of them are unreasonable. But the employee receives the brunt of the emotion from the customer. The situation is particularly bad if the employee cannot provide a satisfactory solution to an urgent problem.

For middle managers, examples of mental intensity are dealing with difficult employees, firefighting, and information overload.

The mental intensity on some jobs is like wading through wet sand. The action needed on this component may involve job design or managerial style, as we will see in the next chapter.

Time Spent on Job

This component refers to the total hours worked by the employee and the degree of control that the employee has over the hours worked.

An example is the employee who must work excessive total hours including desired or undesired overtime. Some undesired overtime is called "voluntary," but nothing could be further from the truth. Another example is working evenings or weekends ("unsocial hours"). At the managerial level, some managers are on call 24 hours per day, seven days a week. Being accessible to employers during "nonwork" time contributes to work overload. The conference call at a bank mentioned previously is a dramatic example. Aside from the mental demands on the individual employees, imagine the effect on the families involved.

Long hours are particularly bad when the employee is not able to occasionally adjust or vary the hours to provide some relief.

To minimize the mental demands, we need to change the process design to eliminate the excessive hours and change policies to provide flexibility on the hours worked.

Job Content

This component refers to the match of job requirements with employee skills and interests.

Let's face it, some jobs are simply boring, repetitive in content, have short job time cycles, have little or no opportunity to learn new skills, or all of these attributes. Some people are comfortable with these jobs and the match is good. Other people cannot handle boring jobs or jobs that they feel are unimportant. Sometimes, technology (as a part of job redesign) can provide automation to do the boring jobs.

A further example is assigning personnel to jobs that underutilize their skills and lead to boredom and a feeling of failure because skills have not been recognized. A final example involves jobs that provide no opportunity for employees to participate in decision making. This means the work procedure is handed to the employee and involves approvals from a supervisor on routine job steps. All of this concerns the "meaningfulness" of the job. To address this issue, the next chapter discusses redesign of individual jobs using the concepts of skill variety, task identity, and task significance.

Another aspect involves the physical exertion and working conditions associated with jobs. Examples include dangerous equipment, exposure to chemicals and air pollution, high noise levels and temperature levels, and other hazardous working conditions. Subtle inferior working conditions also take their toll over time. These span a wide variety and include physical matters such as wrist problems for data entry personnel and lack of immediate private space for workers in crowded workplaces.

Action on this component involves job design for the man/machine interface ("ergonomics" is the five dollar word) and facilities management for the total environment.

Control in Doing the Job

Lack of control in setting priorities, deciding work methods, and the use of resources ranked high in responses to my surveys on the contributors to work overload. Actions on this issue can involve process or job design for self-control, participation of employees in decision making about jobs, and clarifying unclear performance goals and responsibilities – coming up in the next chapter.

Social Interaction on the Job

This component involves how well employees work together as a group.

A pleasant work environment means that co-workers are friendly in their personal interaction and help each other in doing their jobs. Workers must be competent in their jobs so that co-workers are not overloaded because of shortcomings of others. When these factors are weak or missing, then workers start each day with negative feelings that make a work overload situation worse.

Action on this component involves matching job requirements to employee skills by careful selection and training of employees. Again, we need management initiatives.

MENTAL DEMANDS AND POOR MANAGEMENT PRACTICES

The mental demand issues and management practices are shown in Table 5.2.

Table 5.2 Mental demands and management practices.

Management support
- Trust and respect
- Feedback
- Nonfinancial reward and recognition

Career planning
- Job security
- Job lock-in
- Financial compensation

Family-friendly practices
- Demands of work and home
- Flexibility of work schedules
- Childcare and eldercare

Management Support

The support component concerns the organizational environment among management and employees.

The ideal is trust, openness, fairness, and mutual respect among all levels of management and employees. It includes the degree to which supervisors show concern and compassion for personal problems of employees. Such matters cover a spectrum but we all know examples – and the negative ones outnumber the positive ones.

Old Arabic proverb: Arrogance diminishes wisdom.

An example is the lack of timely and constructive feedback to personnel from management. Feedback is essential, but often it simply does not occur because of the fear of confrontation. A further example is the need for nonfinancial rewards and recognition.

Action on this element requires initiatives by management (at various levels including the top level) to provide a positive job atmosphere. The concepts of empowerment and self-regulating work groups (we will discuss these in Chapter 7) are likely contributors here.

Career Planning

This component concerns the various uncertainties that employees have about their current job and the opportunities for the future.

Start with the lack of job security due to mergers, technology, and the general economy. But the uncertainties also include unclear job performance goals and too many changes or new "programs" for which employees are not prepared. Another career uncertainty is "job lock-in", that is, the employee does not see how and when he or she can progress from the current job to a more desirable one.

Personnel are discouraged with jobs that have little opportunity to learn new concepts and develop new skills. Couple this with financial compensation that is not competitive with other organizations and the mental stress becomes serious.

Right or wrong, we live in an environment in which the desire for a high standard of living results in the need for a high family income. This often results in both spouses working – with the many ramifications of work and family overload. It also means that the main breadwinner seeks a career with higher and higher compensation. This component is serious for lower-level employees, middle managers, and professional specialists. Imagine the mental demands on a single mother earning the minimum wage rate. In these situations, we end up with another mental demand (how can I earn more money?) that adds to the total job picture.

Action on this component requires initiatives by all levels of management; job redesign cannot make a major contribution here. It also involves broader work-family issues, which we will discuss in Chapter 11.

Family-Friendly Practices

Often, both spouses work while trying to manage the many, many activities in raising a family and handling the conflicting demands of work and home.

Increasingly, companies find that they must provide work scheduling flexibility and other support such as advice on childcare and eldercare. Thus, work-family programs are now an important element in recruiting and retaining good personnel. Some companies are providing exceptional help to employees; other companies simply don't consider such practices as a company responsibility. We will discuss this issue in Chapter 11, Work and Family Issues.

The mental demands of a job vary greatly for different occupational groups. Karasek and Theorell (1990) provide a thorough discussion for nine typical occupational groups and 44 specific jobs within the groups. The nine groups are managers, professionals, craftsmen, technicians/administrators, bureaucratized service workers, commercialized service workers, routinized workers, laborers, and marginal workers.

It is useful to prepare and conduct a survey of employees periodically to learn how well mental demands are being addressed in jobs. Karasek and Theorell (1990) describe a Job Content Questionnaire that provides questions to evaluate the psychological and social structure of the job – issues such as work demands, decision-making opportunities, and social interaction. The recommended format has 49 questions; a limited version has 27 questions. The scores obtained using the questionnaire can be compared with national averages. The results of such a survey may be surprising.

The demand-control-support (DCS) model developed by Karasek and his associates provides an excellent foundation for a study of job design. Van Yperen and Hagedoorn (2003) extend the Karasek research to investigate the influence of job control and job social support on both fatigue and intrinsic motivation (the pleasure and satisfaction in the job itself). Their study of 555 nurses showed that when the nurses have better job control (for example, making decisions about their work, methods used to carry out work) then this reduces fatigue in highly demanding jobs. Also high levels of job social support produce elevated levels of intrinsic motivation, regardless of job demands and job control. We will examine these issues further in Chapter 6 when we redesign the jobs.

This chapter emphasizes that the mental demands of jobs can be addressed by examining the job content and management practices. But individuals can also help themselves in handling job stress – see Chapter 9 under "Care for the Well-Being of the Middle Manager."

SUMMARY – THREE KEY POINTS

1. Long work hours and excessive mental demands are tightly braided together and can spell disaster.

2. Mental demands on a job can be caused by the work content of the job. You can redesign out some of this static.

3. Mental demands can also be caused by poor management practices. Middle and upper management must pick up the ball on this one.

In the next chapter we discuss how to redesign the processes and jobs to eliminate work overload from two dimensions: 1) provide sufficient time, resources, and other elements; and 2) provide a work content and atmosphere that has reasonable mental demands.

6

How Can We Redesign Work at the Job Level?

> *Sure, the principles in this chapter can help to redesign individual jobs. But don't underestimate the power of people to redesign their own jobs. When they are given the chance to redesign work, they often start with their personal work environment. Examples from my research in manufacturing include eliminating drafts in the work area, reducing the amount of junk food in the vending machines, improving space usage in the parking lot, designing a special work table for operator comfort, improving communication among shifts, and developing a more secure method for attaching tags to work baskets. One person called these examples the "frustrations" of the job. Frustrations cause mental demands that contribute to work overload.*

If management wants personnel to contribute to work redesign, management must first pay some dues by permitting personnel to work on frustration problems. In one manufacturing organization, voluntary workforce teams were formed to redesign work. About 80 percent of the problems selected by the teams were frustration problems. Unfortunately, management directed that the teams only work on problems that would lead to a tangible gain for the company. Soon after the directive, the number of teams dropped from 15 to four.

Three areas of research will help us to redesign work at the job level. These areas are: analysis of job characteristics, analysis of mental demands of jobs, and job design for self-control. This research will not only serve to reduce work overload but also reinvent the fabric of jobs to make them more satisfying and thus provide an additional – and powerful – antidote to work overload.

ANALYSIS OF JOB CHARACTERISTICS

In a classic book, Hackman and Oldham (1980) describe five characteristics that result in more meaningful and satisfying ("enriched") jobs (see Table 6.1).

Table 6.1 Characteristics of "enriched" jobs.

Skill variety
Task identity
Task significance
Autonomy
Feedback

Skill Variety

Jobs should have sufficient variety to use a diversity of employee skills and talents. In designing jobs, we should:

- Use a flow diagram to identify the different tasks.

- Combine different sequential tasks to produce larger work modules for individual employees ("horizontal job enlargement").

- Make provisions for workers to acquire a variety of skills and encourage the rotation of job assignments to use these skills.

Task Identity

Jobs should cover a task from beginning to end and result in a completed visible output. In designing jobs, we should try to:

- Combine tasks so that one person performs all of the tasks required for a complete piece of work.

- Arrange work into meaningful groups, for example, by external customer, by internal customer, or by product or other basis so that workers can personally relate to the work. ("I process the expense accounts for the engineering department").

- Use a self-managing team or other type of team to perform all of the work needed for one type of customer.

Task Significance

Jobs should be important and affect internal and external customers. We should:

- Provide means of direct communication and personal contact among employees and customers.

- Encourage face-to-face contact with customers.

- Arrange for personnel to talk directly with customers about complaints.

Autonomy

Personnel should participate in planning the work. This means:

- Provide greater self-control in decision making.

- Provide authority to make decisions formerly made at higher levels ("vertical job enlargement").

- Encourage personnel to determine work methods.

Feedback

Jobs should provide direct knowledge of results to personnel. We should:

- Create feedback systems, for example, computer support, to provide personnel with information directly from the job itself. Ask personnel how their jobs should be designed to effectively and fairly monitor their performance and give them timely feedback.

- Establish communication channels among personnel and customers.

The first three elements, skill variety, task identity, and task significance, collectively express the meaningfulness of the work. When we design jobs that are truly meaningful, it helps to recruit and retain talented people. Look around your own organization and see if that isn't true.

Next, we will consider work redesign for mental demands.

ANALYSIS FOR MENTAL DEMANDS

We will use the eight categories of mental demands of a job from Chapter 5 to present some principles.

Mental Intensity of the Job

- Ask personnel how their jobs should be designed to relieve mental pressure associated with the jobs. Wrzesniewski and Dutton (2001) make a good case of the benefits of having the employee "craft" their own job. Thus, the employee redesigns his or her job by: 1) changing the number, scope, and type of tasks that make up the job; 2) changing the quality and/or amount of interaction with others encountered in the job; and 3) viewing the job as an integrated whole rather than as a set of discrete work tasks.

- Combine several short activities so that a job has sufficient scope to avoid boredom and help personnel to develop new skills. Design the job so that the person starts and completes the entire product or service to be delivered to the customer. This approaches the old concept of a craftsman – not a wild idea in these days of customized products.

- Watch for opportunities for personnel to communicate with customers and to use judgment in making decisions involving customers. This helps to develop people by providing intellectually challenging activities.

- Design jobs to minimize physical risks such as safety hazards, noise, dust, and other environmental concerns.

- Use technology to do unpleasant or boring tasks.

Time Spent on the Job

- Keep aware of conflicting demands of work and family for personnel and use flexible hours, shared jobs, or other means to ease the burden. Be careful that such steps do not cause a work overload problem for other personnel.

- Watch for work overload problems for supervisors and managers who have responsibility for three shifts seven days per week. Regular monitoring of three shifts plus firefighting on special problems can become a disaster.

- Watch for shift work that includes unsociable hours, no flexibility, or unpredictable hours.

- Watch for the amount of overtime. Even if paid overtime is desired, the result can be a stressed-out person.

- Provide work schedules that recognize personnel responsibilities outside the job.

- Assist personnel who are responsible for the welfare of children, parents, grandparents, or others. Being responsible for others is stressful and personnel need the time and resources to care for others. See Chapter 11, Work and Family Issues.

Job Content

- Help people to see the purpose and significance of the job. Jobs should have a complete, visible output.

- Provide a job scope that encompasses a variety of skills.

- Be sure that the job content is in line with the capabilities of the person and the resources provided.

> ✎ *Old Russian proverb: If your friend is made of wax, don't place him near the fire.* ✎

- Design the physical aspects of the workplace (individual's workplace and community areas) to make the surroundings pleasant. Tackle these issues:
  - Temperature
  - Noise

- Lighting (people prefer natural lighting)

- Chairs and desks

- Hallways (how about colorful hallways with "street signs"?)

- Gathering areas in a central location

- Small quiet places to work as well as team areas for collaboration ("caves and common areas")

- Dress code

Some of the leading companies on workplace design include Amoco, Ethicon Endo-Surgery, Ford Motor Company, Hewlett-Packard, Pitney Bowes, and Steelcase.

Control in Doing the Job

- Clarify job uncertainty and conflict to minimize confusion and frustration. Avoid job designs in which personnel receive conflicting demands from several people.

- Provide personnel with a complete understanding of their responsibility and what they are supposed to do. This includes clarifying overlapping responsibilities with other personnel and conflicting responsibilities to meet various organization goals (for example, quantity of output vs. quality of output).

Lack of control is often cited as a reason for work overload. But "lack of control" is trite. We need to be specific, and later in this chapter you will find checklists for self-control that pinpoint how to redesign a job.

Social Interaction on the Job

- Avoid physical and/or social isolation of personnel. Provide social support by having interaction among personnel during the workday. Encourage people to have a best friend at work and to help each other.

- Add some fun to the job. This can be as simple as posting baby pictures, arranging an ugly tie/ugly shoe contest, or an endless variety of other events. Use whatever type of fun fits your business territory. *Managing to Have Fun,* Weinstein (1996) describes 52 fun events – one for each week of the year. *301 More Ways to Have Fun at Work,* by David Hemsath (2001), is another useful source of ideas. A third source is *Fun Works: Creating Places Where People Love to Work,* by Leslie Yerkes (2001).

- Watch for unusual opportunities to create an environment for social interaction. Dolores Fry is president of Ultimate Home Care, a firm that provides homecare services. At her office, I was greeted not by Dolores but . . . by her dog. The dog comes to work with her each day and roams the offices at will. This may not be feasible in many situations but imagine the tone that this friendly dog sets in the office. That president (an accountant by background) also has a charming novelty in full view in her office – a large doll house. And she had her husband's office (he works for her) decorated with a civil war motif because he is a civil war buff. This is the kind of imagination that we need in our workplaces.

Management Support

- Provide personnel with regular feedback on their performance and support in meeting their job objectives.

- Be accessible to personnel to discuss their job concerns. Don't wait for people to come to you with a problem. Take the initiative to seek out people to show your concern for them as a person. Yes, this will take time.

- Provide personnel with sufficient authority to decide the "how" of doing the work. See Empowerment in Chapter 8. Provide opportunities for people to be creative in helping to design the job.

Career Planning

- Do a thorough job of matching job requirements with personnel skills and interests (see Chapter 7).

- Assist personnel with career planning and development. Try to meet with them quarterly. Periodically, give people the chance to learn new skills. Make sure that each person has someone who encourages their development and cares about them as a person.

- Address company and job uncertainties as quickly as possible. Don't hide behind the excuse that "upper management hasn't told us yet." At least find out a date when information may be available.

- Have the human resources department conduct a salary survey of local businesses to assess whether company salary levels and benefits are consistent with competing firms.

- Strive for fairness in sharing economic rewards by eliminating extreme differences in salary among upper management and hourly personnel.

- Provide reward and recognition for outstanding personnel. This means say something once a week – at least say thanks.

Family-Friendly Practices

- Flexible work schedules

- Assistance in meeting childcare needs

- Assistance in meeting eldercare needs

- Availability of family and medical leaves

- Assistance with physical and mental health needs

- Assistance with other family matters

- Elimination of mandatory overtime

A discussion of these specific practices is presented in Chapter 11, Work and Family Issues.

Volvo Cars made use of Job Design/Health Promotion teams to help detect and resolve psychosocial hazards (Karasek and Theorell 1990; 230). Volvo's efforts at psychosocial job redesign involved both assembly-line workers and white-collar workers. At one plant, a total of eight changes were introduced: 1) offices and workshops rebuilt in a new layout; 2) traditional supervisor role replaced by a more facilitative role; 3) less authoritarian management style; 4) less confrontational style by trade unions; 5) computer aids to improve work efficiency; 6) more personal contact among customers and employees; 7) work organized in teams; and 8) antismoking campaigns. (Karasek and Theorell 1990; Wallin and Wright 1986).

Overall, Karasek and Theorell state it well: the job changes "were all oriented to eliminate unnecessary restrictions in employee decision making, increase intellectually challenging tasks such as customer contacts, and build social cohesion in the work unit. These changes occurred at both the level of the task and at the level of organizational policy in a mutually reinforcing manner."

These principles aim to redesign processes to minimize the time involved in work overload and decrease the mental demands of work overload. We proceed now to redesign individual jobs to provide self-control by those doing the jobs.

ANALYSIS FOR SELF-CONTROL

In Chapter 2, we identified three important perceptions about the causes of work overload: "process not capable. . .", "lack of control in setting priorities," and "unclear performance goals and responsibilities." In redesigning work, the concept of self-control addresses these three causes and other causes of work overload.

Self-control is a universal concept, applicable to a bank teller serving customers, a technician running a chemical reactor, a supervisor running a work unit, a middle manager running an operations department, a plant manager responsible for meeting the various goals set for the plant, or a general manager responsible for running a division at a profit. In our application of the concept, we will focus on the middle manager and the people reporting to that manager. The concept, originally proposed by J. M. Juran in 1962, is applicable to both manufacturing and service jobs.

An ideal objective for designing individual jobs is to place human beings in a state of self-control, that is, to provide them with all they need to meet performance objectives. To do so, we must provide people with:

1. Knowledge of what they are supposed to do

2. Knowledge of what they are actually doing (performance)

3. Ability and desire to regulate the process, with minimum variation

These three elements are basic, but they are far too general. We will dissect them into sub-elements to help us to redesign jobs.

Most job designs do *not* meet the three elements, and subelements of self-control. Some managers proclaim that they "provide people with all the tools they need to do the job." In many cases, this is not true.

"All the tools needed" means the elements of self-control. How do we evaluate for self-control? By applying the following checklists, for the current and proposed job design we can redesign the jobs. These checklists (adapted from Gryna 2001, Chapter 16 and Shirley and Gryna 1998) are not theoretical but are based on my research in talking with people about their jobs. Separate checklists are given for the manufacturing and service sectors. Depending on your interest, see the following checklist for the manufacturing sector or skip to the checklist for the service sector later in this chapter.

CHECKLIST FOR MANUFACTURING SECTOR

The elements and sub-elements of self-control are shown in Table 6.2.

Table 6.2 Self-control in the manufacturing sector.

1. Knowledge of what they are supposed to do
   - Clear and complete work procedures
   - Clear and complete performance standards
   - Superior selection and training of personnel
2. Knowledge of what they are actually doing (performance)
   - Thorough review of work
   - Thorough and timely feedback of review results
3. Ability and desire to regulate the process to meet the standards, with minimum variation
   - A process and job design capable of meeting performance standards
   - Process adjustments that will minimize variation
   - Personnel training in adjusting the process
   - Process maintenance to retain the inherent process capability
   - A strong quality culture and environment

Criterion 1: Knowledge of What They Are "Supposed to Do"

Providing personnel with the knowledge of what they are supposed to do is essential for self-control. The following checklist can help to evaluate this criterion.

Clear and Complete Work Procedures

1. Are there written product specifications, process specifications, and work instructions? If written down in more than one place, do they all agree? Are they legible? Are they conveniently accessible to the worker?

2. Do personnel receive specification changes automatically and promptly?

3. Do personnel know what to do with defective raw material?

4. Have responsibilities in terms of decisions and actions been clearly defined?

5. Do personnel who perform the job have any impact on the formulation of the job procedure?

6. Are procedures "reader friendly"?

Clear and Complete Performance Standards

7. Do personnel consider the standards attainable?

8. Does the specification define the relative importance of different quality characteristics? If control charts or other control techniques are to be used, is it clear how these relate to product specifications?

9. Are standards for visual defects displayed in the work area?

10. Are the written specifications given to personnel performing the work the same as the criteria used by inspectors? Are deviations from the specification often allowed?

11. Do personnel know how the product is used?

12. Do personnel know the effect on future operations and product performance if the specification is not met?

13. Are job standards reviewed and changed when more tasks are added to the job?

14. Do personnel feel accountable for their output, or do they believe that shortcomings are not under their control?

Superior Selection and Training of Personnel

15. Does the personnel selection process match worker capacity (technical, physical, work schedule, mental, emotional) with job requirements?

16. Have personnel been trained to understand the specification and perform the steps needed to meet the specification?

17. Does training include the why, not just the what?

18. Does the design of the training program consider the background of those to be trained?

19. Have personnel been evaluated by testing or other means to see if they are qualified?

Criterion 2: Knowledge of What They Are Actually Doing (Performance)

For self-control, people must know whether their performance conforms to standards on product and process characteristics. Here is a checklist to help evaluate this criterion.

Thorough Review of Work

1. Are gauges provided to the personnel? Do they provide numerical measurements rather than simply sorting good from bad? Are they precise enough? Are they regularly checked for accuracy?

2. Are personnel told how often to sample the work? Is sufficient time allowed?

3. Are personnel told how to evaluate measurements to decide when to adjust the process and when to leave it alone?

4. Is there a checking procedure to ensure that personnel follow instructions on sampling work and making process adjustments?

5. Is a review of work performed at various checkpoints in the process, not just when the work is complete? Is the sample size sufficient?

Thorough and Timely Feedback of Review Results

6. Are inspection results provided to personnel, and does the supervisor review these results with personnel?

7. Is the feedback timely and in enough detail needed to correct problem areas? Have personnel been asked what detail is needed in the feedback?

8. Do personnel receive a detailed report of errors by specific type?

9. Does feedback include positive comments in addition to the negative?

10. Is negative feedback given in private?

11. Are there certain types of errors that are tracked with feedback from external customers? Could some of these be tracked with an internal early indicator?

12. Do upper management and supervision provide the same message and actions on the importance of quality vs. quantity?

13. Where appropriate, is feedback provided to both individuals and a group of personnel? Is time provided for discussion with the supervisor and does the discussion occur?

14. Does feedback include information on both quality and quantity?

15. Where appropriate, are reports prepared to describe trends in quality (in terms of specific errors)? Are such reports prepared for individual personnel and for an entire process performed by a group of people?

Criterion 3: Ability and Desire to Regulate the Process to Meet the Standards, with Minimum Variation

The process given to personnel must be capable of meeting quantity and quality requirements, and the job design must include the necessary steps and authority for personnel to change the process when results are not acceptable. A checklist for evaluating the third criterion of self-control typically includes the following questions.

A Process and Job Design Capable of Meeting Performance Standards

1. Is the process (including procedures, equipment, software, information) given to personnel capable of meeting standards on quality and quantity of output? Has this capability been verified by trial under normal operating conditions? The process must be stable in order to measure the true process capability. On average, there may be enough time to perform a task but unexpected firefighting can still cause overload.

2. Has the quality capability of the process been measured to include both inherent variability and variability due to time? Is the capability periodically checked?

3. Has sufficient time been provided to perform the job taking into account interruptions and delays?

4. When the volume of work changes significantly, do provisions exist to adjust individual responsibilities or add resources?

5. Does the pace of the work allow for personal time and time to discuss the work with supervisors and co-workers?

6. Does the job design minimize monotonous tasks?

7. Has the design of the job made use of the principles of errorproofing?

8. Has equipment, including any software, been designed to be compatible with the abilities and limitations of workers?

9. Has the workplace been designed to be neat and clean? The 5S approach is useful: Sort (only necessary items at the workplace), Set in order (arrange items so that they are easy to find, to use, and to put away), Shine (keep the workplace clean), Standardize (make shine become a habit), Sustain (provide the time, resources, and rewards to continue 5S).

10. Is paperwork periodically examined, and are obsolete records destroyed to simplify working conditions?

11. Are enough personnel cross trained to provide an adequate supply of experienced personnel for filling in when needed?

12. Can personnel institute changes in a job when they show that the change will provide benefits? Are personnel encouraged to suggest changes?

Process Adjustments that Will Minimize Variation

13. Have personnel been told how often to reset the process or how to evaluate measurements to decide when the process should be reset?

14. Is there a process adjustment personnel can make to eliminate defects? Under what conditions should personnel adjust the process? When should personnel shut down the machine and seek more help? Whose help?

15. Have personnel actions that cause defects, and the necessary preventive action, been communicated to them, preferably in written form?

16. Can personnel institute changes in a job that they show will provide benefits? Are personnel encouraged to suggest changes?

Personnel Training in Adjusting the Process

17. Is there a hidden "knack" possessed by some personnel that needs to be discovered and transmitted to all personnel?

18. Have personnel been provided with the time and training to identify problems, analyze problems, and develop solutions? Does this include diagnostic training to look for patterns of errors, and determine sources and causes?

Process Maintenance to Retain the Inherent Process Capability

19. Is there an adequate preventive maintenance program on the process?

20. When personnel encounter an obstacle on the job, do they know where to seek assistance? Is this assistance conveniently available?

A Strong Quality Culture and Environment

21. Is there sufficient effort to create and maintain awareness of quality?

22. Is there evidence of management leadership?

23. Have provisions been made for self-development and empowerment of personnel?

24. Have provisions been made for participation of personnel as a means of inspiring action?

25. Have provisions been made for recognition and rewards for personnel?

Next, we provide similar checklists for the service sector.

CHECKLIST FOR THE SERVICE SECTOR

The elements and subelements of self-control for the service sector are shown in Table 6.3.

Table 6.3 Self-control in the service sector.

1. Knowledge of what they are supposed to do
   - Clear and complete work procedures
   - Clear and complete performance standards
   - Superior selection and training of personnel
2. Knowledge of what they are actually doing (performance)
   - Thorough review of work
   - Thorough and timely feedback of review results
3. Ability and desire to regulate the process with minimum variation
   - A process and job design capable of meeting performance standards
   - Changes in job design
   - Handling problems
   - A strong quality culture and environment

Criterion 1: Knowledge of What They Are "Supposed to Do"

The manufacturing sector makes extensive use of product and process specifications and work procedures, but the use of such documents is still evolving in the service sector. Nevertheless, providing personnel in the service sector with the knowledge of what they are supposed to do is essential for self-control. The following checklist can help to evaluate this criterion.

Clear and Complete Work Procedures

1. Are job descriptions published, available, and up to date?

2. Do personnel know who their customers are? Have they ever met them?

3. Do personnel who perform the job have any impact on the formulation of the job procedure?

4. Are job techniques and terminology consistent with the background and training of personnel?

5. Are there guides and aids (for example, computer prompts) that lead personnel to the next step in a job?

6. Are there provisions to audit procedures periodically and make changes? Are changes communicated to all affected personnel?

7. Are there provisions for deviations from "home office" directives to meet local conditions?

8. Are procedures "reader friendly"?

9. Does supervision have a thorough knowledge of the operations to provide assistance when problems arise?

10. Do procedures given to personnel fully apply to the job they do in practice?

11. Have personnel responsibilities been clearly defined in terms of decisions and actions?

12. Do personnel know what happens to their output in the next stage of operations and understand the consequences of not doing the job correctly?

13. If appropriate, is job rotation used?

Clear and Complete Performance Standards

14. Are formal job standards on quality and quantity needed? If "yes," do they exist? Are they in written form? Do personnel consider the standards attainable?

15. Have personnel been told about the relative priority of quality vs. quantity of output? Do personnel really understand the explanation?

16. Are job standards reviewed and changed when more tasks are added to a job?

17. Do personnel feel accountable for their output, or do they believe that shortcomings are not under their control?

18. Does information from a supervisor about how to do a job always agree with information received from a higher-level manager?

Superior Selection and Training of Personnel

19. Does the selection process adequately match worker capacity (technical, physical, mental, emotional) with job requirements?

20. Are personnel given an overview of the entire organization?

21. Is there regularly scheduled training to provide personnel with current information on customer needs and new technology?

22. Do personnel and their managers provide input to their training needs?

23. Does training include the "why," not just the "what"?

24. Does the design of the training program consider the background of those to be trained?

25. Do the people doing the training provide enough detail? Do they know how to do the job?

26. Where appropriate, are personnel who are new to a job provided with mentors?

Criterion 2: Knowledge of What They Are Actually Doing (Performance)

For self-control, people must have the means of knowing whether their performance meets job requirements. The following checklist can help to evaluate this criterion.

Thorough Review of Work

1. Are personnel provided with the time and instructions for making self-review of their work?

2. Can errors be detected easily?

3. Are independent checks on quality needed? Are they performed? Do peer personnel or others perform these checks?

4. Is a review of work performed at various checkpoints in process, not just when work is completed? Is the sample size sufficient?

5. Is there an independent audit of an entire process to ensure that individual work assignments are integrated to achieve process objectives?

6. Where appropriate, are detailed logs kept on customer contacts?

Thorough and Timely Feedback of Review Results

7. Do upper management and supervision both provide the same message and actions on the importance of quality vs. quantity?

8. If needed, do standards exist on making corrections to output?

9. Where appropriate, is feedback provided to both individuals and a group of personnel? Is time provided for discussion with the supervisor, and does the discussion occur?

10. Is feedback provided to those who need it? Is it timely? Is it personnel specific?

11. Does feedback provide the level of detail needed particularly to correct problem areas? Have personnel been asked what detail is needed in the feedback?

12. Is feedback provided from customers (external or internal) to show the importance of the output and quality?

13. Does feedback include information on both quality and quantity?

14. Is positive feedback in addition to negative (corrective) feedback provided?

15. Is negative (corrective) feedback given in private?

16. Do personnel receive a detailed report of errors by specific type?

17. Where appropriate, are reports prepared describing trends in quality (in terms of specific errors)? Is this done for individual personnel and for an entire process performed by a group of people?

18. Are there certain types of errors that are tracked with feedback from external customers? Could some of these be tracked with an internal early indicator?

19. Are personnel held accountable for errors? Are goals for the number of errors established and communicated to personnel?

A credit card provider has identified 18 key processes such as credit screening and payment processing. For these 18 processes, more than 100 internal and supplier process measures were identified. Daily and monthly performance results are available through video monitors and are posted. Each morning, the head of operations meets with senior managers to discuss the latest results, identify problems, and propose solutions. Employees can access a summary of this meeting via telephone or electronic mail. The measurement system is linked to compensation by a daily bonus system that provides up to 12 percent of base salary for nonmanagers and 8 to 12 percent for managers (Davis, Rosegrant, and Watkins 1995).

Criterion 3: Ability and Desire to Regulate the Process with Minimum Variation.

The process given to personnel must be capable of meeting quantity and quality requirements, and the job design must include the necessary steps and authority for personnel to change the process when results are not acceptable. Here is a checklist to evaluate this criterion:

A Process and Job Design Capable of Meeting Performance Standards

1. Is the process (including procedures, equipment, software, information) given to personnel capable of meeting standards on quality and quantity of output? Has this

capability been verified by trial under normal operating conditions?

2. Has sufficient time been provided to perform the job taking into account interruptions and delays?

3. Does the pace of the work allow for personal time and time to discuss the work with supervisors and co-workers?

4. Has the design of the job made use of the principles of error proofing?

5. Has the workplace been designed to be neat and clean? The 5S approach is useful (see previous under "Manufacturing Sector").

6 Does the job design minimize monotonous or unpleasant tasks?

7. Have provisions been made in the job design to anticipate and minimize errors due to normal interruptions in the work cycle?

8. Can special checks be created (for example, balancing of accounts) to detect errors?

9. Can steps be incorporated in data entry processes to reject incorrect entries?

10. Does the job design include provisions for action when wrong information is submitted or information is missing as an input to a job?

11. Is paperwork periodically examined and obsolete records destroyed to simplify working condition? Thus, the need for an adequate records management policy.

12. When volume of work changes significantly, are there provisions for adjusting individual responsibilities or adding resources?

13. Are there external factors (for example, no account number on a check, cash received instead of a check, and so on) that hinder the ability to perform a task?

14. Are some personnel cross-trained for different tasks to provide an adequate supply of experienced personnel for filling in when needed?

15. If appropriate, is a "productive hour" scheduled each day in which phone calls and other interruptions are not allowed, thus providing time to be away from the work location to attend to other tasks?

16. Has equipment, including any software, been designed to be compatible with the abilities and limitations of personnel?

17. Is there an adequate preventive maintenance program for computers and other equipment used by personnel?

18. Is there a hidden knack possessed by some personnel that needs to be discovered and explained to all personnel?

19. For a job requiring special skills, have personnel been selected to ensure the best match for personnel skills and job requirements?

Changes in Job Design

20. Are proposed changes limited by technology (for example, address fields on forms)?

21. Can personnel institute changes in a job when they show that the change will provide benefits? Are personnel encouraged to suggest changes?

22. What levels of approval by management are required for proposed changes to be instituted? Could certain types of changes be identified as not needing any level of management approval?

23. Do management actions confirm that they are open to recommendations from all personnel?

Handling Problems

24. Have personnel been provided with the time and training to identify problems, analyze problems, and develop solutions? Does this include diagnostic training to look for patterns of errors and determine sources and causes?

25. Are personnel permitted to exceed permitted process limits (for example, maximum time on a customer phone call) if they believe it is necessary?

26. When personnel encounter an obstacle on a job, do they know where to seek assistance? Is the assistance conveniently available?

A Strong Quality Culture and Environment

27. Is there sufficient effort to create and maintain awareness of quality?

28. Is there evidence of management leadership?

29. Have provisions been made for self-development and empowerment of personnel?

30. Have provisions been made for participation of personnel as a means of inspiring action?

31. Have provisions been made for recognition and rewards for personnel?

These checklists are long but they provide the necessary level of detail to redesign jobs.

REDESIGN FOR WORK AND FAMILY LIFE – CASE EXAMPLES

Friedman, Christensen, and DeGroot (1998) propose a threefold approach for redesigning work: 1) clarify what's important – both business goals and personal goals; 2) recognize and support the personal goals of employees; and 3) analyze the work processes (a main theme of this book) and search for ways to redesign the work to achieve business goals and enable employees to pursue personal goals. It sounds good, but it also sounds difficult and time consuming. But they cite persuasive case examples to encourage us to take a shot at trying.

At a pharmaceutical manufacturing plant, a 24-hour command center monitors more than 10,000 "hot spots" such as fire alarms, sewage lift stations, and a hazardous manufacturing process. Shifts change 21 times each week and exchanging information among members from different shifts is cumbersome. Of course, the midnight to 8:00 a.m. shift is frequently difficult to fill. Operating conditions, including the wearing of protective clothing, make the work stressful. Also, the number of hot spots will increase by 50 percent within the next year. The director's first step was to call his staff together and explicitly define the business goals of the command center. He also acknowledged that the workload might have a negative impact on employees' personal lives, and he asked them to describe to one another what that impact would be. Then he asked his staff to redesign a solution to the scheduling problem that met both business needs and personal requirements. No solution was out of bounds as long as it met both business needs and personal requirements.

Their solution: work 12-hour shifts, three days on and four days off one week, four days on and three days off the next week. The redesign far exceeds expectations. The benefits: information exchange occurs seven fewer times reducing errors during shift transfers, overtime is less, other operating efficiencies result. In addition, the new schedule allows employees to meet their personal needs in ways not possible under the old system. The new schedule even creates a high demand to work in the command center.

In another example, a new department director at a food services company was able to redesign to meet both business demands and employee personal needs. She inherited an administrative assistant who had a reputation of being unmotivated and cynical and caused poor morale. Some people suggested that she be fired.

When the two of them first met, the director learned that the assistant liked to work with numbers, but her lack of computer experience prevented her from doing finance work. Also, the assistant was caring for her mother who had a terminal illness.

The two worked together on redesigning the process to improve department performance and recognize the personal needs of the assistant. As a result of a recent consolidation, the assistant was maintaining separate budgeting and inventory control systems. The assistant was then trained in Excel and in basic analytical methods giving her greater control over the department's finances. Managers could receive and interpret the information faster. The morale and performance of the assistant improved notably; she could even work from home when her mother needed more attention.

Yes, managers may resist this three-step approach because they believe it will be time consuming. Surprisingly, the researchers concluded that this is not the case. Recognizing personal priorities can be integrated in the activity of improving the work process. The researchers suggest three ways for managers to begin: 1) apply the steps to one employee; 2) initiate some small team meetings to discuss work and personal life goals; and 3) apply the steps to the managers themselves. Of course, there will be obstacles to using this approach, but imagine the potential benefits.

SUMMARY – THREE KEY POINTS

1. Five characteristics of individual jobs determine the meaningfulness and satisfaction of a job.

2. Principles are available to redesign jobs to address eight categories of mental demands.

3. Checklists can help to redesign jobs for self-control. These checklists are not academic stuff but come from research combed from the real world of jobs.

In the next chapter, we will discuss matching people with the job design.

7

How Do We Match Work to People?

Terry Carter is a perfect example of the right person for the right job. She is a nurse who draws blood from patients in a hospital test laboratory. Her day begins early – even before the full laboratory staff appears. Terry not only draws the blood from the arm, she also handles the paperwork. The job has mental demands – patients arriving all day long, sometimes overflowing the lab, patients who don't read the instructions on a sign, patients with the wrong paperwork, patients who are physically sensitive to the drawing of blood, patients who want to personally verify their name on the vial and so on. All this plus many interruptions. But, day in and day out, Terry does her job with wonderful competence and a smile and personal manner that puts patients at ease. Sure we can, and should, redesign the work. Better yet, we should ask Terry to redesign the work. What a lady.

WHY MIDDLE MANAGERS SPEND MOST OF THEIR DAY ON "PEOPLE PROBLEMS"

One cause of work overload is a poor match among job requirements and employee attributes, that is, people are in the wrong job.

One study estimated that 27 percent to 40 percent of people are in the wrong job (Wood 1994). This is a key reason why many middle managers say that they spend most of their time on "people problems." Managers won't solve these problems with the brief medicinal enchantment of scotch whiskey.

The skills required by a job may be inherent in a person or may be acquired by training or experience. The matching of employee skills (inherent or acquired) with job requirements is essential for two reasons: 1) to meet quality and quantity requirements of the job, and 2) to provide for employee well-being.

Thus, we must address selection, training, and retention of personnel.

WORK OVERLOAD AND SELECTION OF PERSONNEL

Some firms have a thorough process of selecting new employees. For example, Southwest Airlines accepts only 4 percent of 90,000 applicants each year. Chick-fil-A refuses to grow faster than it can recruit excellent store operator candidates. The payoff? At Chick-fil-A turnover of store operators is less than 5 percent compared to the 30 percent-40 percent common in that industry (Reichheld 2001). (The cost of hiring a new employee is $10,057 in recruiting and administrative expenses, according to the Employment Management Association).

Perhaps your firm knows how to recruit and assign people to positions – but many firms simply don't. Better employee selection can reduce work overload in several ways:

- Reduce the work overload for middle managers who must spend time on the "people problems" that arise because people are in the wrong job.

- Reduce the work overload for those employees who must carry more than their fair share of work because of the deficiencies of a colleague.

- Achieve better employee satisfaction and help to retain key employees.

- Provide better service to customers.

We know that we should not recruit people just to fill open personnel requisitions, but pressures sometimes force us to do just that. But selecting the right person for the right job is easier said than done, so let's address some key issues.

Organizations need many types of people – managers and supervisors, individual contributors, those working in informal or formal teams, customer contact people, back office operations people, to name a few. Increasingly, many jobs involve the collection, analysis, processing, and dissemination of information. We are in an era of the knowledge worker who receives and processes information rather than the physical worker who relies primarily on physical strength.

The five attributes for most positions are shown in Figure 7.1.

Personality is one important attribute for many (but not all) positions. This attribute is increasingly essential as organizing by teams becomes more important. A chemical manufacturer even places job applicants in a team problem-solving situation as part of the selection process. Larry Silver of Raymond James Financial states the case well: "We need to recruit people who play well in the sandbox with others, that is, don't throw sand in people's face and

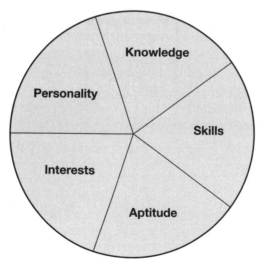

Figure 7.1   Attributes for a position.

do work together to build castles." Mutual respect and support among employees is indispensable if we are to lessen work overload due to job content and mental demands.

One time-tested tool for classifying personality types is the Myers-Briggs Type Indicator (McDermott 1994). This indicator describes 16 personality types that are based on four preference scales: extrovert or introvert, sensing or intuition, thinking or feeling, and judgment or perception. Thus, one (of 16) personality types is an extrovert, sensing, thinking, and judgment person. Organizations need all 16 types of personality. Analyzing responses to questions on the indicator from prospective employees helps to determine the personality types of individuals. Then they can be assigned to positions to get a good fit of jobs and personality. The key is to hire for fit of person and position, rather than just filling the open position. Then we must guide the employee to move from success to success in that position as a stepping-stone to an even more desirable position. The payoff is a better chance of successful performance by the individual – and a satisfied employee because he or she likes the job. Also, getting the right fit of people and jobs assures that employees contribute their fair share to the workload; a poor fit leads to work overload for others in the same department. Many skills can be taught, many personality characteristics cannot.

Other personnel assessment tools are available to evaluate aptitude, knowledge, skills, personality, and interests. A good reference is Morgan and Smith (1996). If assessment tools might be useful to you, ask your human resources department to recommend the specific tools you need. These tools are an investment to select people who will meet job requirements but also be happy in the job.

The position description plays an important role in the selection process. The description should include the knowledge, skills, abilities, and personal characteristics (KSAP's) for the job along with a summary of the responsibilities, working hours, and travel required. Ideally, the job description should contain a list of the specific decisions and actions that the incumbent is expected to perform. Sears goes beyond the usual position description and includes such matters as decision-making authority, future competencies gained while in the position, possible next jobs, and recommended minimum time in the position.

If job descriptions don't exist, ask someone to draft a description for the next open job. You then review the draft and finalize. If you don't have time, just think of the time spent on problems with people in the wrong jobs.

Also, remember that the work you originally hired a person to do may no longer exist. Likely, these people have been shifted to other jobs – those in need of being filled. But the result may be that there are now people in jobs for which they really are not suited. This is no one's fault; it's just a reality. So, you need to review jobs and redistribute work to maximize the match among people and jobs.

Raymond James Financial takes a more proactive approach. They encourage their people to request a change in position, if they desire. The only condition is one year of experience before requesting a new position. The result is an environment in which job changes are a normal activity.

Job satisfaction factors include career development and satisfaction with job content. At best, we can do an imperfect job on these factors. The fault may be management; the fault may be the employee. Some employees are viewed as highly competent but are simply not satisfied in the job. Is there anything we can do? Yes, we can encourage them to apply for a transfer to another position. Raymond James prides itself in employee selection – carefully matching job requirements with the knowledge, interests, aptitude, and skills of an applicant. But an employee's interests may change with time. So a policy exists that says, after an employee has been in a position for one year, the employee may apply for a position in another function. Sometimes, the examples are dramatic, for example, a bond trader transfers to a marketing position. Further, managers are encouraged to support employees who apply for a transfer. The policy has worked so well in practice that both managers and employees see the benefits and actively support the concept. Managers now realize that losing an employee from, say, operations or MIS to another function not only means a more satisfied employee but it has an unexpected benefit – the employee brings the experience of operations to the new function and explains to the new colleagues why operations must do activities in a certain way. Over time, this helps to build up a surprising amount of empathy among functions. Tim Eital of Raymond James says "transfers are the greatest thing" because people are comfortable with reapplying if the position with their new company has not been satisfactory.

Finally, on matching skills and interests to job requirements let's realize that the worst situation on work overload is when a job does have work overload *and* the employee has neither the skills nor the interest in the job. Disaster. When a job does have work overload but there is a good match of the job with the person then at least the good match helps the person to roll with the overload problem. But back to basics – we need to study the process and the job to eliminate the work overload *and* we need to have a good match of the job and the person.

Morgan and Smith (1996) is an excellent source of proven ideas for the entire staffing process.

WHAT TO DO WHEN PERSONNEL REQUISITIONS CANNOT BE FILLED

In my surveys, the number one cause of work overload was insufficient resources to handle even the normal workload. Sometimes, this is due to a lack of approval to hire sufficient people. But sometimes management has given approval, but talented people simply cannot be found. For example, the absolute number of workers aged 25 to 34 has declined 12 percent since 1990. Some companies don't have the problem of finding people, but other companies face a severe problem. Finding talented people is hard work. The actions to take are summarized in Table 7.1.

Table 7.1 Finding the right people.

1. Study the work processes for simplification
2. Benchmark other organizations
3. Analyze the recruiting process
   - Redesign the recruiting process for simplification
   - Ask upper management to form a taskforce
   - Track the recruiting process
4. Review recruiting sources
   - Build a special rapport with selected educational institutions
   - Hire retirees
   - Rehire former employees
   - Use special sources of personnel
5. Outsource the work
6. Use unusual working time arrangements
7. Use remote locations for some personnel
8. Institute innovative employee policies

Let's now examine these actions.

1. Study the process that requires additional people for simplification and redesign (see Chapter 3). Perhaps waste can be eliminated from the process or some tasks automated

so that additional resources are not necessary. If no one has time to study the process, consider using the unused salaries to hire a consultant for studying the process. Or, get help from a local school to have a student study the process.

2. Benchmark other companies on compensation, benefits, and other aspects of employment. If your company is not competitive, you simply won't be able to attract good people. Period. The benchmark information can convince your management of the need to meet competition. Some websites provide supplementary data on labor information:

   • Bureau of Labor Statistics: www.bls.gov

   • Employment Policy Foundation: www.epf.org

   • Economic Policy Institute: www.epinet.org

3. Analyze the recruiting process itself. The Rogers Corp. did exactly that to reduce the time required filling positions – an average of about 78 days with a range of 132 days (Leonard 1986). They collected data for each of the steps in the process. This approach identified two problems: the time to find the right resumé or person and, surprisingly, the time required to move the candidate through the other steps in the process.

   • Ask upper management to form a taskforce to analyze the recruiting process, set numerical goals on recruiting, and develop a recruiting strategy to meet those goals.

   • Set up measurements to track performance of the recruiting process, particularly as it affects work overload. These measurements might include time to fill positions, number of applications generated, time required to generate applicants, quality of interviews as rated by interviewees, and number of jobs filled with people who remain at least one year. Design these measurements to meet the needs of your organization.

4. Review recruiting sources. The usual sources are internal sources (promotion from within, employee referrals), advertising, Internet, public and private employment services, schools, and job fairs. But more innovative methods are needed. One example involves schools. Instead of having job openings posted in a career center at a

school, speak with faculty. Build a rapport with that faculty by helping the faculty strengthen the education program for example, guest speakers, field trips, summer employment for faculty, and sponsorship of faculty professional travel. Setup student internships or a cooperative education program in which students alternate between school and work. This is a long-range effort that can provide a continuing supply of students. Kodak is a role-model company for this approach.

- Consider hiring some retirees from inside or outside the company – even on a part-time basis.

- Former employees. Sometimes, employees leave a company and then discover that leaving was a mistake. After a few months, they can be contacted to inquire about their satisfaction in their new job. This keeps a contact available for possible reemployment. Some organizations have alumni websites that help to keep in touch with former employees. The cost of rehiring is only about half as much as the original hire, and rehires tend to remain twice as long, according to the Society for Human Resource Management.

- Don't forget special sources of personnel – people with disabilities and "welfare to work" programs are two examples. Provide personal transportation to people who have no means of transportation. McDonald's found that furnishing transportation helped them to recruit employees. Another unusual source is prison labor, that is, having your work performed inside a prison.

5. Outsource the work. Outsourcing is the process of subcontracting to an external supplier an activity that is currently conducted in house. Estimates suggest that at least 85 percent of major corporations now outsource some activities. Outsourcing has advantages and disadvantages. My bottom line is that the core (key) activities must be carefully identified within each organization, and once identified they should be performed internally and not be outsourced. But other activities are candidates for outsourcing – particularly if people cannot be recruited. The Servicemaster Co. is an example of an organization that does outsourcing work (for example, facility maintenance)

and turns dead-end jobs into a career path while providing help to their client organizations.

6. Consider unusual working arrangements for workers, for example, flexible hours, telecommunication work, working on and then off for periods of time. We discuss these arrangements further in Chapter 11. Management must use caution when providing special working arrangements for certain workers to accommodate their family needs. The other workers who put their time in on the job every day at regular hours are invariably affected by the flexible hours given to certain workers. The result can be an extra work burden for those who are not on flexible hours (and this impact is usually not voiced by the regular employees because they are trying to be cordial co-workers). The concept of flexible hours is excellent, but when employees with children are on flexible hours, these employees need to realize that flexible hours make scheduling more difficult particularly when the inevitable happens – the babysitter doesn't show up, the unexpected carpool problem, the medical emergency. Thus, employees who are on flexible hours need to understand that co-workers and supervisors are affected and need to be shown some appreciation.

7. Consider the use of remote locations for some personnel. Pacific Bell has a department called Virtual Office Development to organize telecommuting. People work from their homes, customer sites, or neighborhood telework centers. When they need to come to the office, they are assigned a desk and phone calls are routed to that desk.

8. Institute innovative employee policies. Examples are: pay an employee who is on another employer's health plan through a spouse, a mentor for every new employee, a credit union, pastoral care, car wash at work, birthday movie tickets. The search for innovative policies should focus on employee needs, and thus employees should be asked for ideas.

Some specialties have a persistent staffing shortage, for example, information technology (IT). In January 2002, a chief information officer magazine survey reported that nearly two thirds of IT executives agreed that they are experiencing an IT skills crisis with the largest shortages in application development, project management, and networking. Although there is no lack of IT job applicants, traditional recruiting practices have not been able to supply personnel with the right set of skills.

WORK OVERLOAD AND TRAINING OF EMPLOYEES

Training of employees is essential to prevent errors and process waste that in turn leads to work overload. But work overload and training can have some unusual scenarios.

A bank provides an example. Ordinarily, an operations department has a full-time training person. But what happens when the department is not able to handle the volume of work that must be processed each day? The manager does what any manager would do in those circumstances, that is, the manager assigns the trainer to do operations work rather than training work. This results in overload for the trainer plus someone who was scheduled for training does not get trained adequately.

Another example also involves operations. When operations people are in training for one or more full days the department is left short-handed and the result is work overload. Experience suggests that training be done in three-hour segments using small class sizes so that sufficient people remain in the department to handle the normal activity without work overload.

Another example concerns the influence of downsizing on training. When organizations reduce the number of employees, the impact on training takes several forms. Some training positions are eliminated and the training activity is absorbed by regular personnel probably as an "add on" to their regular job – resulting in work overload. But another form surfaces at the supervisor/manager level. If the downsizing eliminates some supervisor/manager positions then other supervisors/managers must absorb the managerial responsibility (including training) previously performed by those whose positions have been eliminated – again causing work overload. Or, the downsizing may result in a lower-level employee being promoted to a higher-level position that requires training and resources. But perhaps the person best able to give that training is a supervisor/manager who is gone because of downsizing (Ligos 2001).

Providing training to update skills is also an obvious step to take. For example, 96 percent of Graniterock employees say that they receive training to further themselves (*Fortune* 100 Best Companies). Why not institute job rotation to develop people to have a wide variety of skills and maybe to provide a respite from boring or stressful jobs. Cummins Engine rotates managers through several different specialties before finalizing a role.

Progressive companies make an investment in training. The January 12, 2004, issue of *Fortune* on the "100 Best Companies to Work For" reports these scores on training hours per year: an average of 49, a high of 162, and a low of 12. The leaders are Container Store, Paychex, Edward Jones, and AFLAC. If they can make that investment, why not other companies?

WORK OVERLOAD AND RETENTION OF KEY EMPLOYEES

When workers leave an organization, those remaining usually experience work overload to make up for the resources lost. In addition, the process of hiring replacement workers involves time spent by middle management to find job applicants, conduct interviews, select the new employees, and provide training for these new workers. All of this results in work overload for middle managers. Looking at this from a cost standpoint is also dramatic: according to one estimate, the cost of losing a key employee is between one to two times the employee's salary and benefits. Thus, the retention of experienced employees is an important preventive measure for work overload. In the latest *Fortune* ranking (January 12, 2004) of the "100 Best Companies to Work For," the top 10 companies were J.M. Smucker, Alston & Bird, Container Store, Edward Jones, Republic Bancorp, Adobe Systems, TD Industries, SAS Institute, Wegmans Food Markets, and Xilinx (Levering and Moskowitz 2004).

Employees remain with an organization because they are satisfied with their jobs. But job satisfaction covers many factors. My research suggests that the key elements of job satisfaction are shown in Table 7.2.

Although this list provides the key factors that apply in most organizations, you need to know what the key factors are in your organization, the relative importance of each factor, and how well the organization is performing on each factor. Ask your employees, by using a carefully designed and administered survey or a focus group of employees, with a trained focus group facilitator.

Table 7.2 Job satisfaction factors.

- Financial compensation
- Employee satisfaction with job content
- Career development
- Trust, openness, and mutual respect among management and employees
- Empowerment and participation in decision making
- Workload
- Feedback and support from management
- Cooperation among employee
- Nonfinancial forms of recognition
- Other factors

My research says that financial compensation is still a key factor in job satisfaction – no surprise. Salaries for managerial personnel are usually higher than those for nonmanagerial. Sometimes, a sobering scenario arises: a nonmanagerial person reaches the top of a salary scale, desires more salary to meet family needs, and therefore wants to become a manager. But you know what may happen: we lose a wizard chemist, programmer, or customer representative . . . and gain a lousy manager. Then, we no longer have a good match of skills and job and the person becomes unhappy because of marginal future rewards in the managerial job.

A promising approach is called the "dual career ladder" concept of employee development. In this concept, people in nonmanagerial positions (often technical) can advance higher and higher as a specialist. At the top levels of being a specialist, the person can make as much or more salary than the person's supervisor. Examples of titles for this position are Fellow or Distinguished Engineer. One of the pioneers of the dual ladder approach was Esso Research and Engineering Company. Other companies that practice this approach are 3M, IBM, and Texas Instruments. Some organizations also experiment with spiral career paths that create opportunities for employees to switch periodically among management, professional, and entrepreneurial positions within a company. Still other organizations try lattice career paths that make use of cross-functional and cross-project activities. These innovative approaches are alternatives to the traditional hierarchical and bureaucratic career paths. Again, an excellent reference is Morgan and Smith (1996).

Any of the aforementioned job satisfaction factors (or more likely a combination of factors) can lead to an employee leaving.

Where work overload and stress are present, then the likelihood of a departure becomes imminent. Thus, it is essential that over-worked, stressed personnel be identified and steps taken to alleviate the condition. The symptoms of work overload discussed in Chapter 1 can be helpful in making this identification. Burnout surveys are also available (see Maslach and Leiter 1997).

Motivational approaches to "fire up" employees do not work unless the basics of a good job environment (the job satisfaction factors) are in place. Some motivational approaches can even be harmful if employees believe that an approach is only short term. Motivational techniques cannot be plugged in to make up for deficiencies that are more basic.

    ◁ *Old Chinese proverb: Talk doesn't cook rice.* ▷

If the basics were not in place, the money spent on motivation programs would be better spent on correcting the deficiencies. If the basics are in place, then motivational techniques can make a useful contribution by supplementing the foundation of a good job environment.

Workplace flexibility (see Chapter 11) is a powerful retention tool. A 2003 survey conducted by the WFD consulting firm revealed that 86 percent of Deloitte and Touché client service professionals cited workplace flexibility as important. This enabled Deloitte and Touché to avoid about $27 million in turnover costs in fiscal 2003.

Finally, we must say the obvious. Recognition of employees is basic. Whatever the forms of recognition they must be both tangible and intangible. Don't forget to have upper management participate. As John Kritsas of Raymond James says, "Getting upper management involved in the recognition has big emotional value."

Measures of Retention

Three types of information are useful in retaining key employees: retention data, employee opinion survey results, and outside research information. Operating without this information is like flying blind.

Keeping track of retention data helps to identify problem areas and provide data for convincing upper management to institute required actions. Measures of retention can include:

- Percentage of employees who chose to leave their jobs

- Percentage of employees who were dismissed from their jobs

- Percentage of employees who rated jobs as highly satisfactory

- Other

Data can be analyzed by gender, age, length of time with the company, departments, job categories, and performance levels of employees. Comparing the data to the average for your industry gives you a scorecard.

To gain a better understanding of retention data, an employee opinion survey is also helpful. Questions might include, "Are you encouraged to balance work and personal life?" "Are pay and benefits competitive with other organizations?" "Are you satisfied with career opportunities in the organization?" "Do you participate in decision making in your job?" These are examples and you need to design the survey questions to fit your organization needs. Bank One and the Gallup organization are collaborators on a survey for the bank operations people.

A third set of information to understand retention is research to learn from other organizations. An easy place to start is the survey reported by *Fortune* on the "100 Best Companies to Work For." The survey reports specific examples of personnel policies and practices that enable an organization to achieve the "Best Company" citation. Human resource specialists in a company should periodically meet with their counterparts in other companies to exchange ideas on personnel policies and practices.

Thus, the combination of retention data, employee opinion surveys, and outside research provides the information needed to develop plans for retention of key employees. Baptist Health Systems of South Florida uses these three sources of information (Gustafson 2001).

SUMMARY – THREE KEY POINTS

1. Most companies do not adequately match employee skills, aptitudes, and interests with job requirements. That's why middle managers spend most of their day on "people problems."

2. Recruiting and retaining truly talented people is hard work, but innovative approaches can help to achieve success. You can get those open personnel requisitions filled with the right people.

3. Sure, training costs time and money. But it helps to keep talented people in a company. Being stingy on training leads to a stagnant workforce.

Now that we have a good match of people and jobs, let's be sure that we tap all of the talents of those people. That's the subject of the next chapter.

8

How Do We Achieve Participation and Empowerment of Employees to Reduce Work Overload?

At a company with highly successful workforce team activity, the manufacturing manager proclaimed, "I had always felt that these new approaches were not my management style. My thinking had been that the guys out in the shop knew what's wrong and what to do about it. My style was to beat them on the head hard enough to make them do it."

I asked why he started workforce teams, and he replied, "I don't know. It just hit me." Thanks to his support and the humanistic approach used, workforce teams are now a clear success in the company. When defects decreased, and usable output increased, he became a fan of teams. He says, "Workforce teams have caused me to rethink my old style of managing."

EXCITING IDEAS FOR ORGANIZING WORK

Many businesses are still chilled by a climate of fear. But it's changing. Management is learning how to mesh the interaction of the two systems we need to meet objectives: the technical system (design, equipment, procedures) and the social system (people, roles).

New ways of organizing work, particularly at the workforce level, continue to emerge. For example, supervisors are becoming "coaches;" they teach and empower rather than assign and direct. Operators are becoming "technicians"; they perform a multiskilled job with broad decision making rather than a narrow job with limited decision making. Team concepts play an important role in these new approaches. Basic to all this are the concepts of participation and empowerment. During the past two decades, the quality movement in America has taught us many lessons about participation and empowerment. The ideas in this chapter draw upon those in my book *Quality Planning and Analysis* (2001).

ONE MORE TIME – PARTICIPATION AND EMPOWERMENT

Participation of the workforce is essential to analyze and change processes to eliminate work overload. One plant manager says: "No one knows a work place and a radius of 20 feet around it better than the worker."

But will the workforce resist such participation because it could result in a loss of jobs – themselves or someone else? Yes, it's a natural reaction. Management must hit this head on, that is, guarantee that no jobs will be lost due to the process analysis. It can be done – and it has been done. For example, at the Baxter Healthcare plant in Mountain Home, Arkansas management promised that employees involved in any jobs that were eliminated would be transferred to another line in the plant (*Fortune* 2001).

The one exception to a policy of no job loss is a decrease in sales revenue because adequate sales revenue is essential for company survival.

EMPOWERMENT

Empowerment goes a major step beyond participation – it brings democracy to the workplace, after years of autocracy. Empowerment is the process of delegating decision-making authority to lower levels within the organization. Particularly dramatic is empowerment of the workforce. But empowerment goes far beyond delegating authority and providing additional training. Empowerment means encouraging people to take the initiative and broaden their scope of activity;

empowerment also means management being supportive if mistakes are made.

As employees become more empowered in their work, the feeling of ownership and responsibility becomes more meaningful. Further, the act of empowering employees provides evidence of management's trust. Additional evidence is provided when management shares confidential business information with employees. For many organizations, such steps are clearly a change in the culture and help to reduce the mental demands of jobs.

Empowerment is important because: 1) the higher education level of the workforce results in a desire and ability of the workforce to participate in decision making; 2) many repetitive jobs are now done by technology and the remaining jobs require skills and judgments by the workforce; and 3) the importance of meeting customer needs often requires employees to make immediate decisions when dealing with customers. Thus, empowerment has the potential of providing opportunities for the workforce. All of this can result in a positive outlook about their jobs by the workforce and thus reduce the negative mental demands that often come with work overload.

But implementing empowerment is not easy, so we offer first some realities and then some working rules to follow. First, the realities.

The Realities of Empowerment

- Contrary to what they say, many middle managers and supervisors fear empowerment. They don't want to give up their authority to subordinates, particularly when the middle managers are accountable for the results. Further, they wonder what their role is. They have grave doubts about the new approach. They will not express their concern if higher management is clearly in favor of empowerment (instead, "wait six months, this fad will pass"). Middle managers need to be encouraged to understand empowerment.

- Contrary to what they say, many workers fear empowerment and some will choose not to participate. Some want the authority but don't want to be held accountable. As empowerment provides more and more authority, the scope of responsibility and accountability becomes more intense. Let's face facts: if you are receiving $8-$10 per hour you may view empowerment as resulting in additional stress (that you observe every day in your supervisor) or the additional risk if your participation does not yield positive results. Some people prefer that the work be laid out for them (including decisions) and not be concerned with decision making. Some people view the decision making as additional mental demands (see Chapter 5). But most people view the decision making as positive to relieve some of the mental demands of the job. We need to recognize these differences among people. Don't try to make them all fit one mold.

- True empowerment requires a fundamental change in management style – from command and control to participation. For some companies, such a basic change may not be possible now – or ever. Some highly profitable companies practice empowerment, but other highly profitable companies are strictly command and control companies.

From realities, we proceed to guidelines for implementing empowerment.

Guidelines

- Both for middle management and for workers, be specific about the goal of empowerment and provide policies concerning execution and limits on the authority being delegated.

- Expect to spend money to develop the knowledge, skills, and expertise of people.

- Empower only those employees who demonstrate that they have the knowledge and skills to make certain decisions. Do not empower other employees until they have made that demonstration. Making this distinction among employees will not be easy.

- Provide support and understanding to middle managers who truly use empowerment to delegate authority to subordinates.

- Hold periodic meetings of managers (before problems arise) to confirm the approach and offer suggestions for improving the decision making for the future.

- Expect requests for additional salary and rewards from those who are now empowered to use their knowledge and skills. These requests are appropriate – because the jobs have changed. Management should take the initiative and provide the salary increases.

- If appropriate, give employees some control of financial and other resources including such matters as hiring and firing employees.

- If appropriate give employees access to customers, suppliers, and higher management.

Wetlaufer (1999) describes a dramatic example of empowerment at AES Corporation, a global electricity company. The characteristics include organization around teams to run operations and maintenance, elimination of functional departments, every person a generalist (a "mini-CEO"), and upper management acting as advisors. Sure this is radical . . . but it has been done.

The Changing Roles

With empowerment comes the need to redefine the basic roles of upper management, middle management, and the workforce. One model at a bank looks like this:

- Upper management acts as shapers and coaches. As a shaper, it creates, communicates, and supports the organization's mission. As a coach, it helps when asked but avoids entering the day-to-day problems of middle management.

- Middle management not only runs its area of responsibility but also works as a group to integrate all parts of the organization. In addition, it supports the workforce by eliminating obstacles to progress.

- The workforce is the primary producer of the output for customers. Its closeness and knowledge about its work means that it uses its empowerment to determine how the work can best be done.

Mann (1994) explains how managers will need to develop skills as coaches, developers, and managers of activities that reside in different departments ("boundary managers").

Note, how essential it is for management to provide employees with the information, feedback, and means of regulating their work, that is, meeting the three elements of self-control is a prerequisite for empowerment and subsequent motivation. Self-control includes the training needed to make good decisions under empowerment. Empowerment requires employees to have the capability, the authority, and the desire to act.

Empowerment is not new, but we have many lessons to learn from previous experience. Some good references are Argyris (1998) and Forrester (2000).

TEAMS, TEAMS, TEAMS

Some organizations report that, within a given year, 40 percent of their people participate on a team; some organizations have a goal of 80 percent.

Aubrey and Gryna (1991) describe experiences with more than 1000 teams during four years at 75 banking affiliates of the Bank One Corporation. The average team size was seven members, with a range of two to 11. On some teams, membership was assigned; on other teams, membership was voluntary. Although the focus was customer satisfaction, reduced costs, and increased revenue two other benefits emerged – a reduction in work overload in specific jobs and improved communication among front-line employees and management.

Teams may be ad hoc to address one problem or may be permanent to be responsible for a specific activity. Next, we examine the three types of teams (see Table 8.1): project teams, workforce teams, and self-managing teams.

Project Teams

A project team (sometimes called a cross-functional team) usually consists of four to eight persons (managers, professionals, and workforce) who are drawn from multiple departments to address a selected problem. The problem can be work overload.

The team meets periodically, and members serve part time in addition to performing their regular functional responsibilities. When the project is finished, the team disbands.

The project team consists of a sponsor (upper management), a leader, a recorder, team members, and a facilitator. Details about these specific roles can be found in Gryna (2001), Chapter 8.

Table 8.1 Summary of types of teams.

	Project team	Workforce team	Self-managing team
Purpose	Solve cross-functional problems	Solve problems within a department	Plan, execute, and control work to achieve a defined output
Membership	Combination of managers, professionals, and workforce from multiple departments	Primarily workforce from one department	Primarily workforce from one work area
Basis and size of membership	Mandatory; 4-8 members	Voluntary; 6-12 members	Mandatory; all members in the work area (6-18)
Continuity	Team disbands after project is complete	Team remains intact, project after project	Permanent
Other names	Improvement team	Employee involvement group	Self-supervising team; semiautonomous team

Source: Gryna, Frank M. 2001. *Quality Planning and Analysis, Fourth Edition.* The McGraw-Hill Companies. Used with permission.

An example of a special project team is the "blitz team." A blitz team is a project team that operates on an accelerated problem-solving schedule (several weeks for a solution rather than several months). This is accomplished by having the team meet more frequently – several times a week, often for full days. A full-time facilitator may be assigned to the team. Additional help is provided for data collection and analysis. Most of the diagnostic work (data analysis, flow charting) is done outside of the meetings. Skiba (1996) describes the application at the Mayo healthcare system.

Workforce Teams

A workforce team is a group of workforce-level people, usually from within one department, who volunteer to meet weekly (on company time) to address problems that occur within their department. Team members select the problems and are given training in problem-solving techniques.

Kaiser Permanente uses Quality in Daily Work Teams. These front-line work teams focus on work process improvements. The projects span across departments and include both clinical and support services (Centano, Ahn, and Tawell 1995).

Where the introduction of these teams is carefully planned and where the company environment is supportive, they are highly successful. With respect to work overload, the benefits of teams fall into two categories: 1) identifying and eliminating wasted effort in processes so the time saved can help to reduce work overload, and 2) addressing the mental demands and psychosocial issues involved in many jobs. Teams can use the self-control checklist of questions (see Chapter 6) given previously to analyze the jobs. This analysis can then lead to ideas for job redesign. The workers can immediately institute some of the job changes; other changes will need to be presented to managers for possible modification, changes in procedures, changes in physical work environment, and then implementation.

If project teams or workforce teams are to be formed to analyze work overload, the process should evolve carefully and slowly. You should start with one or two pilot teams assisted by a facilitator. These pilot projects are critical to prove that the workforce can make an important contribution to reducing work overload.

A key question is: if work overload is a problem, how will we provide people with the time and skills to study their jobs? These teams should meet during regular working hours. Only middle management and upper management can authorize the time and training to study work overload. It simply won't happen without management support (see Chapters 9 and 10).

Perhaps the most important benefit of workforce teams is their effect on people's attitude and behavior. The enthusiastic reactions of workers, sometimes streaked with emotion, are based on their personal involvement in solving problems (Gryna 1981 provides many examples from a variety of companies). As applied to work overload, the effects can be:

Teams increase the individual's self-respect. At Woodward Governor, a worker spoke highly of teams because "the little guy can get in on things."

Teams increase the respect of the supervisor for the workers. At Pontiac Motor division, a supervisor remarked, because of teams, "I find that I talk more with workers on the line."

Teams increase the workers' understanding of the difficulties faced by supervisors. As a result of team activity, workers for the first time become aware of the supervisor's many burdens. This fosters a more understanding attitude when the supervisor is unable to solve problems quickly. Sometimes, we may even hear a murmur of appreciation for the supervisor.

Teams increase management's respect for workers. An upper manager said: "Some of the presentations by workforce teams have been better than those of my staff people."

Teams change some workers' negative attitudes. At one company, a worker stated, "I always had a chip on my shoulder around here because I didn't think the company cared about the worker. As a result of my team, I've got a lot better attitude."

Teams reduce conflict stemming from the working environment. The removal of work environment frustrations (draft in a work area, a water fountain not accessible to workers, poor food in a vending machine) not only eliminates sources of conflicts, but worker involvement in the removal process encourages them to think that they can deal with other mental demands as well.

Teams help workers to understand better the reasons why many problems cannot be solved quickly. For instance, certain process changes at the Henry, Illinois facility of the BF Goodrich Chemical Group required approval of the Chemical Group technical function located in another city. Workers at the plant could understand the need for this and have subsequently learned why this approval process required some time because of many other process changes being considered.

With all the potential benefits of workforce teams, the success rate has been mixed. Baker (1988) provides perceptive recommendations for management to support and sustain workforce teams. These are:

1. Recognizing and rewarding (not necessarily monetarily) workers' efforts, even if recommendations are not adopted. Giving workers increased discretion and self-control to act on their own recommendations is an excellent reward.

2. Offering monetary rewards through the suggestion program (which may have to be modified to accommodate joint submission by team members).

3. Providing sufficient training to expand worker skills to take on projects that are more complex.

4. Establishing a system for teams to expand into cross-functional teams when it appears to be a logical step. Teams may become "fatigued" when they feel they have accomplished about all they can by themselves and see the need to work with their internal suppliers and customers.

5. Training of middle managers in team tools and techniques so they can ask their subordinates the "right questions" and not be "outsiders." These tools are also useful for the managers' own processes.

6. Addressing middle management resistance when diagnosed. Typically, management is concerned about a loss of authority and control.

7. Measuring effectiveness by focusing on the quality of the process—for example, the training, the group discussion process, the interpersonal relationships, supervisory leadership style—rather than outcomes (for example, reduction of scrap and costs). If the process is right, the outcomes will be also and that will reinforce employee involvement, as well as management commitment.

Every organization must provide for the participation of the workforce in solving problems. One approach makes use of workforce teams. A more revolutionary approach involves self-managing teams.

SELF-MANAGING TEAMS – REVOLUTION IN THE WORKPLACE

A self-managing team is a group of people who work together continuously to plan, execute, and control their work to achieve a defined output. That definition starkly contrasts with the traditional system of work design developed by Frederick W. Taylor, an industrial engineer. Basic to the Taylor system is the division of an overall task into narrow specialized subtasks that are assigned to individuals by a supervisor. The supervisor then coordinates and controls the execution and handles the general supervision of the workers. Taylor's system achieved spectacular increases in productivity and was a major contributor to the affluence during the 20th century. But Taylor's major premise – low level of worker knowledge – has become obsolete by the remarkable rise in education at all levels including the workforce.

Historically, Taylor is viewed as a technocrat, not a humanist. His emphasis on the technical did not go unnoticed by other industrial engineers. Henry L. Gantt, Lillian Gilbreth, and others sought to temper the technical with the humanistic aspects of work design. As a result, organizations increasingly use the education, experience, and creativity of the workforce.

Here are two examples of self-managing work teams:

In an electronics plant, an assembly team handles all aspects of a customer order: it receives the order, prepares the components, assembles and solders circuit boards, tests the boards, ships the boards, monitors inventory levels, and processes all paperwork.

At an insurance company (the Aid Association for Lutherans), work was originally organized into three areas – life insurance, health insurance, and support services such as billing. Under the new organization design, teams of 20 to 30 employees perform all of the 167 tasks that formerly were split among the three functional sections. Now, field agents deal solely with one team. The result is a shorter processing time for cases – and less work overload.

The American Express Consumer Card Group uses "semi-autonomous work teams." A team consists of 10 to 12 employees in the natural work group. Team members do customer service work and manage quality, inventory, and attendance; prepare work schedules; and prepare production reports and forecasts. Individual roles are defined to handle these team responsibilities. The team leader focuses on coaching, feedback, and special human resource issues.

One fast-food firm creates teams of "crew members" (workers at one location) who are trained to manage the site without a full-time manager (Harvard Business School 1994). Not only does this mean installing on-line sensor technology such as the time to prepare an order, but it also means providing crew members with the same operating and financial information provided to a restaurant general manager to run the site. Crew members make operating decisions such as ordering food materials. Thus, knowledge that long separated "brain workers" from "hand workers" now resides in a computer on the operations floor.

The Ritz-Carlton Hotel Company uses self-directed teams. These are process teams aligned with the way customers come in contact with the hotel: 1) prearrival team; 2) arrival, stayover, and departure team; 3) dining services team; 4) banquet services team; and 5) engineering and security team. In a self-directed work team, members may have individual roles but the team shares accountability for meeting performance goals.

A contrast of features of the traditional organization of the workforce and self-managing teams is given in Table 8.2.

Table 8.2 Comparison of organizational forms.

Feature	Traditional organization	Self-managing team
Scope of work	Each individual is responsible for a narrow scope	Team is responsible for a broad scope
Job categories for personnel	Many narrow categories	A few broad categories
Organizing, scheduling, and assigning work	Primarily by supervisor or staff	Primarily by team
Measuring and taking corrective action	Primarily by supervisor or staff	Primarily by team
Training provided	Training for task assigned to individual	Extensive training for multiple tasks plus interpersonal skill training
Opportunity for job rotation	Minimum	High because of extensive training
Reward system	Related to job, individual, and seniority performance	Related to team performance and scope of skills acquired by individual
Handling of personnel issues	Primarily by supervisory personnel or staff	Many issues handled by team
Sharing of business information	Limited to non-confidential information	Open sharing of all information

Source: Gryna, Frank M. 2001. *Quality Planning and Analysis, Fourth Edition.* The McGraw-Hill Companies. Used with permission.

The difference is revolutionary. Workers are empowered to make certain decisions previously reserved for a supervisor.

Clearly, the implementation of such a fascinating but radical approach will be like walking through a minefield. Some key steps involved are:

1. Get upper management to commit to the approach and to accept some unknown risks.

2. Provide in-depth orientation and participation of upper management, middle management, specialists, workforce, and union officers.

3. Analyze the production workflow to define logical segments for teams.

4. Define the skills required, levels of skills, and requirements for certification.

5. Form teams and train the teams and individuals.

6. Develop production goals for teams and provide continuous feedback of information to teams. Such feedback must have the content and timeliness needed to control the process.

7. Change the compensation system to reflect the additional skills acquired by individuals.

8. Develop trust among management and the workforce, for example, the sharing of financial and other sensitive information on company performance.

9. Develop an implementation plan spanning about three years and starting slowly with a few pilot teams.

Some middle managers will have a new job. That new job may be working with a self-managing team but perhaps now as a member, facilitator, or technical consultant instead of the hierarchical supervisor. Such a change in a role affects power, knowledge, rewards, and status and, thus, will be threatening. Organizations have a responsibility to explain the new roles for managers clearly and to provide the training, understanding, and patience to achieve success.

Self-managing work teams are not always successful. For some managers, supervisors, and workers, the demands of the concept are more than they are willing to accept. But self-managing teams can be highly effective if they fit the technology, are implemented carefully, and the people in the organization are comfortable with the concept.

Although these various types of teams are showing significant results, the reality is that, for most organizations, daily work in a department is managed by a supervisor who has a complement of workers performing various tasks. This is the "natural work team" in operations. But team concepts can certainly be applied to daily work. One framework for a team in daily operations work is the control process. As applied to daily work, the steps are: choose control subjects, establish measurement, establish standards of performance, measure actual performance, compare to standards, and take action on the difference. When the natural work team of the department is trained in these concepts, the work team gains greater control over the key work processes so that they can meet customer needs and reduce work overload.

At Bank One, employees are encouraged to use measurements ("metrics") to manage their work. Thus, a subdepartment of 12-20 employees will have their own "Q board" (Q for Quality) of measurements that they manage. They track whatever they feel is important. Their manager may offer suggestions, but the board "belongs" to the employees. They do weekly or biweekly production management reviews to monitor progress of the metrics. The metrics are also used to identify potential projects for a team.

YES, WE CAN MAKE TEAMS EFFECTIVE

The scars of experience provide some principles to follow:

- Provide sufficient time for team members to participate. On a cross-functional project team, members usually spend 15 percent to 20 percent of their working time to attend meetings and do the follow-up work after the meetings. This means about one day each week. Unless sufficient time is provided for people to be on a team, their team activity will be viewed as an "add-on", that is, they must somehow do their work on a team in addition to their regular job. The result is surely work overload – and the regular job doesn't get done and the team activity is weak and results in failure of the team.

- Teams often require a "facilitator." Although not a member of the team, the facilitator plays an important role in helping the team leader. The roles include assistance in team building, training the team members, providing technical support, and helping to solve human relations problems among team members.

◁ *Old French proverb: Soft words don't scratch the tongue.* ▷

Organizations that do extensive team problem solving have several levels of facilitators. In the Six Sigma approach, three levels are employed: a master black belt is usually a full-time facilitator and trains black belts and green belts; a black belt is full time and trains and assists the project team in problem solving; a green belt is part time and helps the black belts.

- Understand that team performance depends on the performance of individuals. Thus, the individuals must understand the common goals, must be able to continuously develop their individual capabilities, and must feel that they are being treated fairly by others on the team. A facilitator can help team members to work toward these characteristics. A useful reference is Avery, Walker, and Murphy (2001).

My research on workforce teams identifies what it is that members like about being on a team. They like:

- Discussing and solving problems as a team

- Presenting their solutions to problems

- Getting engineers and others interested in their problems and working with them

- Freedom to express themselves

- Influencing decisions about their work

- Recognition

- Reduction of conflicts in the work environment

What workforce people like about teams also applies to middle managers and professional specialists.

For a discussion of research conducted on teams, see Katzenbach and Smith (1993).

The humanists in the business world are now swimming in rhetoric – participative management, empowerment, situational leadership, social capital, people building, and industrial democracy. Will management nurture these concepts to help humanize the workplace and further the objectives of all organization members? Time will tell.

SUMMARY – THREE KEY POINTS

1. Participation and empowerment of the workforce can produce ideas to reduce work overload. We need their help.

2. We enjoy – revel in – team sports. Why not use more teams in the workplace? Teams can analyze the technical content and the mental demands of work to reduce work overload.

3. Experiment with new forms of organizing work. If all of the experiments are successful, you aren't being imaginative enough. Take some risks.

Participation and empowerment are not pills that will eliminate the need for more substantial medicine on work overload. That medicine must come from the doctor (upper management). But first, the role of middle management – the next chapter.

9

How Can Middle Managers Handle Work Overload in Daily Operations?

Sometimes software bugs can raise havoc for operations managers and professional contributors. The software usually worked, but on Thursday some unusual transactions caused a failure.

So, they are sorting checks at a bank (three million checks accounting for $2.5 billion per day) and sending some checks to other banks. The computer system keeps track of the number of checks, and the amounts, sent to each bank. Yes, it's critical that the transactions financially balance.

Three subject-matter experts are trying to identify the cause of the failure. While that was going on, other people must manually reconstruct where the checks were going, with amounts, to 400 different banks.

Late Thursday, the system was finally fixed. It blew up again on Friday. Friday and Saturday were hectic until the root cause was found and corrected. Imagine the work overload.

This chapter discusses work overload issues for middle managers and individual professional contributors.

WHO ARE MIDDLE MANAGERS?

We will focus on middle managers, particularly those in operations – the heart of any manufacturing or service organization. Operations managers direct the activities that generate sales revenue through the product or service provided to external customers. They are responsible for meeting various "performance goals" (with or without adequate resources).

For organizations of moderate or larger size, middle managers are often two levels below the CEO and one or two levels above individual workers. Examples include a manager in a bank, a production manager in a plant, a site manager at a construction site, a store manager, a restaurant manager, a manager at an insurance company, a manager at a call center, and many, many more.

Middle managers are the backbone of an organization. They are problem solvers – roll up their sleeves and get the work done. As they are close to day-to-day operations with customers, front-line employees, and suppliers, these middle managers continuously face operating problems.

Downsizing and mergers often lead to a reduction in middle managers. Running lean also can result in fewer layers of middle managers. These and other factors lead to work overload for middle managers. An upper manager remarked to me that middle managers have a more stressful role than upper managers because middle managers have people coming at them from above and below.

REVIEW OF CAUSES OF WORK OVERLOAD

First, we will review the key causes of work overload from Chapter 2.

- Insufficient resources to handle the normal workload (see the following under Personnel Issues)

- Firefighting on problems (see the following under Firefighting)

- Lack of control in setting priorities, deciding work methods, and use of resources (see the following under Departmental Planning and Administration)

- Work process not capable of meeting quantity and quality requirements (see the following under Firefighting)

- Unclear performance goals and responsibilities (see the following under Departmental Planning and Administration)

- Inputs from internal/external suppliers – missing, wrong, late (see the following under Firefighting)

- Inadequate selection and training of personnel (see the following under Personnel Issues)

- Information overload – e-mail and other (see the following under Information Overload)

- Computer hardware or software problems (see the following under Firefighting)

- Other (for example, sustaining change/direction)

No wonder most middle managers, and the people working for them, have work overload. Before we examine these causes in more detail and the action needed, we will first review the role of teams in work overload.

HOW MIDDLE MANAGERS CAN USE TEAMS TO REDUCE WORK OVERLOAD

Chapter 8 discusses how teams can analyze processes and the individual jobs in processes. Many processes are cross-functional, that is, the individual jobs within the process reside in different functional departments, each having its own middle manager. Also, problems within cross-functional processes often occur during the transfer of work among departments (that is, the "white space" on the organization chart). Additional problems occur due to other issues, for example, misunderstandings, different priorities, and lack of feedback between departments. All of this suggests that the middle managers in the process need to form a team of managers (or their representatives) to study work overload in the process. The team would use the concepts discussed in Chapters 3, 4, and 5. Some manager must take the initiative to form the team.

Workforce-level teams using the concepts discussed in Chapters 3, 4, 5, and 6 can analyze individual jobs within a process. The department manager would set up these teams. The caution in Chapter 8 needs to be repeated here. Some middle managers have a background of managing that has established them as bosses – "I'm not bossy, I just have better ideas than you." Many middle managers see a conflict between the boss role and workers participating in solving problems. Managers who are autocratic cannot be expected to embrace the concept of participation. They fear the loss of their authority and think that workforce teams would be a waste of time – and add to the work overload. But we've come a long way in the past two decades – many middle managers now understand that the worker on an individual job knows that job better than anyone else and can contribute valuable ideas.

Next, we address the causes of work overload by examining where middle managers spend their time and how they can reduce work overload for themselves and for their people.

WHERE DO MIDDLE MANAGERS SPEND THEIR TIME?

Middle managers told me that they spend most of their time on six activities:

- Departmental planning and administration

- Firefighting

- Personnel issues

- Meetings

- Managing information

- Business travel

Some middle managers don't even have the time to do all of these activities. For many operations managers, a typical day is this: manage fires, attend high-priority meetings, and read e-mails in the time that remains. What's missing is managing the work process. That's easier said than done, but it's critical and we will address that issue in Chapter 10 under Long Range Actions. But first, let's help middle managers keep their heads above water by discussing the short-range actions needed to reduce work overload.

We start by addressing the major categories of time spent by middle managers.

DEPARTMENTAL PLANNING AND ADMINISTRATION

The issues here are time management, setting priorities, focus, delegation, fun on the job, and having a plan of palliative actions.

Time Management

This will not be a lecture on time management techniques – but those techniques really are useful. Browse in a bookstore and select a book that seems to fit your territory. Hindle (1998) is concise, readable, and practical. Beyond the techniques, my recommendations are:

- Keep a time log for a representative month to estimate the time spent in various work activities such as the six listed previously. Trust me, your memory is not accurate on where you spend your time. The results of a time log will provide some surprises. An alternative to keeping a detailed time log is the work sampling study. Work sampling is the process of recording the frequency of observations in various activities in order to estimate the time spent in each activity. For elaboration, see Aft 2000; Chapter 8.

- Add 20 percent to any estimate you make to complete a project. You need that cushion to allow for the unexpected, which always occurs.

- Schedule a half hour a day for uninterrupted quiet time for collecting your thoughts and assessing priorities. This quiet time may be in the office behind a closed door, taking a walk outside around the property, or in an exercise mode. Later in this chapter we will take a closer look at the importance of exercise.

This may make you laugh. Some mavericks use exercise for creative thinking time. (Medical people say that exercise kicks in the "endorphins.") A lap swimmer (me) enters the water with one problem in mind. After 15 minutes of lap swimming, one to five creative thoughts occur to him. After he leaves the pool, he immediately writes the thoughts down before they are forgotten.

Setting Priorities on Major Projects

Most of us put off working on the difficult problems. Life is more pleasant working on easier problems (those that we can conclude in a short time), those that are of personal interest and fun to us, those in response to a squeaky wheel – a pest who barks the loudest. Thus, sometimes we are working on the wrong problems.

When we work on lower-priority problems, then the important ones fester and become worse – sometimes resulting in a crisis. Instead, we need to set clear priorities based on companywide priorities set by upper management. See Chapter 10 for an example from Bank One. Stick to your priorities and be prepared to tell people how your priorities flow down from company priorities. For complex problems, break up the problem into parts and work on one or a few parts at a time. This shows visible progress and gives you a feeling of accomplishment.

About twice a year, middle managers should step back and review current projects. Then relative priorities must be assigned to the projects. (This is not the same as deciding priorities on firefighting). How to define the relative priorities on major projects is a personal matter but some possibilities are:

- Distinction: "Urgent" must be done now but "important" may have higher value to the organization. Focus on what's really important (I know "they're all important"). With work overload, the middle manager says, "I'm trying to decide how to get the work done, much less solve problems." See below under Firefighting for an important distinction between sporadic and chronic problems.

- Separate the projects into A, B, and C piles where A is the number one priority.

- Hartman (1983) describes an approach at AT&T that makes use of a "Pareto priority index" (PPI) to evaluate each project. The index is:

$$\text{PPI} = \frac{\text{savings x probability of success}}{\text{cost x time to completion (years)}}$$

Table 9.1 shows the application of this index to evaluate five potential projects.

Table 9.1 Ranking by use of Pareto Priority Index (PPI).

Project	Savings, $ thousands	Probability	Cost, $ thousands	Time, years	PPI
A	100.0	0.7	10.0	2.00	3.5
B	50.0	0.7	2.0	1.00	17.5
C	30.0	0.8	1.6	0.25	60.0
D	10.0	0.9	0.5	0.50	36.0
E	1.5	0.6	1.0	0.10	9.0

Source: Juran Institute, Wilton, CT www.Juran.com. Used with permission.

High PPI values suggest high priority. Note how the ranking of projects A and C is affected when the criterion is changed from savings alone to the index covering the four factors.

In deciding priorities, it is important to review with customers, internal and external, the relative importance of current work. (Your most important internal customer is . . . your boss). Customer priorities do change. When the change in priorities is radical, the customer will speak up; when the change is modest, the customer may be silent, but the change needs to be known because of the impact on many matters including work overload.

Stepping back to make a departmental assessment, identifying projects, and assigning priorities takes time, but it's strategic planning at the departmental level. Some middle managers claim that they don't have the time (is this an excuse because they have never been taught how to step back?), but to move ahead in an organization they must somehow find the time.

Focus

Once priorities are set, then the key element is focus. That is, concentrate on a goal and follow through with sufficient energy to complete the task. Bruch and Ghoshal (2002) believe that the most effective managers practice the combination of focus and energy. Their research shows that only about 10 percent of managers are highly effective or "purposeful" (highly focused and highly energetic); about 40 percent are "distracted" (highly energetic but unfocused); 30 percent are "procrastinators" (low focus and low energy); and 20 percent are "disengaged" (high focus but low energy). This explodes the myth that hard work alone yields superior results. Further, the research concludes that although focus and energy are personal characteristics, upper management can directly affect manager behavior by encouraging managers to eliminate waste (the subject of this book) and encouraging managers to develop their own ways to achieve goals rather than rely on formal procedures. Staying focused includes saying "no."

Politely say "no" to people who habitually ask for help on short notice. Let's face it, some people procrastinate and then realize that they need an input from you. Their request becomes "urgent" (to them). The result is work overload for you. It's not fair to you and they need to break their practice of imposing on your good nature. Here's how. Give them a future date and, if this is unacceptable to them, firmly state that the short deadline is impossible to meet. Doing this once or twice will send them a message. Of course, this also means that you must give adequate notice when you are the one making the request.

Finally, learn to say "no" to new work. Politely refuse requests to perform additional work. If you find you must say "yes," then give a date of completion that is realistic (and includes an allowance for the unexpected, which will occur). If the date is unacceptable (to a boss) then propose what current activities will receive a lower priority.

Delegate

Delegate is the name of a song that managers hear all the time. Many managers (particularly rookies) know they should delegate but they are fearful. For example, will the job be done correctly?

Trust your people, empower them, and delegate tasks. Part of work overload of middle managers is due to a failure to delegate.

Sometimes, managers unwittingly encourage reverse delegation. This occurs when a subordinate comes to a manager for help on a problem. When the manager says "I'll get back to you on that," the responsibility transfers from the subordinate to the manager. If this happens with many subordinate problems, the manager becomes overwhelmed. Of course, part of the role of the manager is to help subordinates. But the manager must emphasize that the problem is still the responsibility of the subordinate. The key is empowerment, that is, make sure the subordinate has both the desire and the knowledge and tools to solve the problem.

Add Fun to the Job

We can at least relieve the agony of work overload by keeping a sense of humor. Weinstein (1996) provides 52 ideas; for example, transform a cubicle, take a trip to the toy store, distribute stuffed animals, design personalized fortune cookies.

The holidays furnish plenty of fun outside of working hours. That's great, but sometimes the first day back at work can be a drag on everyone. Thus, it's a good idea if that first day back can be a "recovery day." My friend, Andy Rivera, is manager of a successful restaurant and he tries to have the restaurant closed on the day after a holiday where the employees traditionally have a fun, but exhausting, holiday. Some would say that closing a restaurant for a day is not practical – Andy closes the restaurant.

A Plan of Palliative Actions to Relieve the Overload

Have a plan of palliative (medical word) actions to take when work overload cannot be reduced. Such actions might include special time off, extensive reward and recognition, inserting fun into the work, rejuvenation ideas (see later in this chapter) and a target date for eliminating the work overload. Palliative actions treat the symptom rather than the cause, but they are better than no action.

FIREFIGHTING

In Chapter 2, the second most important cause of work overload was firefighting on problems.

- Distinction: sporadic vs. chronic problems.

  - A sporadic problem is a sudden, negative change in operating results. Examples are an irate customer, a bad batch of material from a supplier, an unexpected absence of a worker, and a computer breakdown in the middle of the night in a department processing checks. Often, we drop what we are doing and address the problem. This is firefighting. Sporadic problems are often dramatic, require a response to a customer or higher management, and get attention. Sporadic problems cause sudden additional work overload – on top of the usual work overload.

Ironically, people who are good firefighters become heroes and are rewarded accordingly. A vice president at a utility once (half jokingly) told me that his organization probably had some "arsonists" who wanted to become heroes. Some people even thrive on firefighting – to them, it's fun and they experience a sense of accomplishment. But it adds to work overload.

– Chronic problems are long-standing negative situations that are not addressed for various reasons. Examples are work processes that are not capable of meeting quantity and quality requirements, unclear performance goals, poorly trained personnel, and information overload. They are not even regarded as problems but are accepted as part of the business environment. Thus, they are not dramatic and receive little attention (until some maverick brings them to life). Chronic problems also cause work overload because of the extra time spent correcting errors, doing excess inspection, and other activities to live with the problem. Solutions to chronic problems are rarely easy to find and implement; otherwise, we wouldn't have the problems. For chronic problems, we need a project-by-project approach where each project is a chronic problem. A project team identifies the cause of the problem, eliminates the cause, and takes steps to prevent the cause from recurring. The approach particularly fits cross-functional problems that often include suppliers – both internal and external. Computer problems during operations are one of many examples. We will discuss the project-by-project approach in Chapter 10 under Developing a Strategy on Work Overload.

The fog of firefighting not only contributes to work overload but it robs us of the time to correct the chronic problems that are a continuous cause of work overload. Firefighting on sporadic problems will always be with us, that is, the irate customer, the call from upper management. Have you heard this from managers? "I know I should be working on the chronic problems but I have no time to do that because I'm spending all of my time firefighting." Thus, we need to address the problem of firefighting in general.

The real answer on firefighting is to prevent the fires (problems) from occurring. That doesn't happen in most companies because there isn't the time to thoroughly plan the work processes (but there is the time to fight the fires when they occur).

> *Old Italian proverb: It is too late to come with
> the water when the house is burned down.*

Meanwhile, what can we do in the short range to do some firefighting but minimize the effect on work overload? Here are some ideas:

- Add temporary help to assist on firefighting. But what if no funds or resources are available? Then the problems accumulate until the situation becomes so serious that management finally allocates funds – or transfers employees temporarily from another department. This is a bad situation, but that's the price we pay for letting a smoldering fire turn into a three-alarmer.

- Train additional firefighters. Sometimes, personnel at lower levels can be trained to handle some of the sporadic problems thus freeing up other resources to handle the more complex problems.

- Face the reality that some problems will not be solved. This means assigning priorities to problems with the emphasis on solving external customer-related problems or problems that come from senior management. (Of course, in both cases, the problems may not really be of the highest priority). But problems with a low priority will probably never get solved. Again, a bad situation.

Bohn (2000) presents a valuable paper on firefighting. His ideas cover both the short range ("tactical") and long range ("strategic"). Smith (1998) describes root-cause analysis and other forms of diagnosing underlying causes of problems.

PERSONNEL ISSUES

Middle managers spend much time on issues involving the people who work for them. Here, we will address matters concerning work overload of those employees:

- Middle managers need to recognize the symptoms of work overload for themselves plus of the workforce. This includes not only the hours worked but also the mental demands of many jobs that can turn long hours into an intolerable situation (see Chapter 5).

- Tim Eitel, senior vice president of Raymond James, purposely plans work so that if a person has work overload for several weeks the person is then assigned a different kind of work for a few weeks to rejuvenate the senses. That different kind of work might be training for themselves, teaching others, or whatever activity the person likes to do. This approach helps to make the work overload period more tolerable. People can handle the overload (temporarily) if they can look forward to a breather. Later in this chapter we will discuss the concept of rejuvenation.

- Have an automatic follow-up on the status of open personnel requisitions.

- Pursue special additional resources such as part-time help form local schools, retirees, or other resources. Consider an outside consultant (paid for from unused personnel budget) to study key processes for waste.

- In far too many companies, we make staffing decisions based on the low part of the product demand cycle, that is, as product demand increases we add overtime or add people – but never enough to cause worry about staffing when demand drops. Unfortunately, as demand grows, we often overload our star people with extra work. That's simply not fair to them. This must be pursued as part of a long-range strategy (discussed in Chapter 10) for reducing work overload.

- Where job responsibilities are not clear, a useful approach is to make a list of specific decisions and actions that the employee must do on the job.

- Chapter 7 emphasizes the importance of selecting people for jobs based on matching the job requirements with the skills, aptitudes, and interests of the person. This is critical in situations of work overload. When people are not matched well to jobs, then work overload can become serious because of the added mental demands placed on the people. Jobs in the operations function often have work overload and are therefore candidates for this situation.

- A useful approach is encouraging employees to request a transfer to another position. This concept has much value even if work overload is not a problem (see Chapter 8). But it does provide one alternative under a work overload situation to prevent a bad situation from becoming worse. Note that it means that the middle manager involved must view this approach positively rather than viewing it as losing a person in a situation that might make the overload problem worse.

- Chapter 7 discusses the importance of training all personnel – not just initially but throughout their career. When people are temporarily placed in training to learn some new concepts those people remaining in the department may have to carry an extra workload until the training is finished. Proper planning of the training can prevent a work overload situation. Judith Lyons of Plan Vista Solutions has some practical suggestions: use three-hour training segments instead of full-day sessions, and keep the class size small to minimize the impact on the department.

- Middle managers must meet department goals and care for the career development and well being of the people in the department.

- Managers can easily spend 20 percent of their time on employee-related benefits, regulations, paperwork, and the many day-to-day problems that arise. An increasing number of organizations are outsourcing their employee relation's activities. This can include payroll and benefits but also hiring, training, job placements, and layoffs. That's a radical change from the past. The organizations handling the employee relation's activities are sometimes called professional employee organizations (PEOs) or professional guilds. This trend may accelerate as the number of temporary and contract workers increases and as the knowledge-based economy demands more and more knowledge workers. A benefit of outsourcing employee relations is to reduce the time spent by internal management on many employee-related activities. But the risk is that relationships with employees will be weakened and career development and company loyalty may suffer. Drucker (2002) presents the pros and cons of this developing concept.

It is also important to pursue the actions discussed in previous chapters: Chapter 5 concerning the mental demands of jobs of subordinates (lack of management support, career concerns, and lack of family-friendly practices) and Chapter 7 concerning retention of key personnel (retention data, employee opinion surveys, and outside research).

MEETINGS

Let's set the record straight – some meetings are necessary, and some are not worth the time spent.

Here are some tips on meetings:

Consider alternatives to a meeting. These include e-mails (ugh) and conference calls. Also, no meetings on Fridays. Many times on conference calls people get "caught" multitasking, that is, the person is reading e-mails during the conference call and is asked a question. Often, the person says, "I'm sorry, could you repeat that." That's a polite way of saying, "I was reading e-mails and not listening to the conference call."

Prepare thoroughly for the meeting. When appropriate, circulate a written agenda before the meeting. This should be one page and list the attendees along with the topics to be discussed and persons responsible, time allotted for each topic, and any key decisions to be made at the meeting.

Conduct the meeting efficiently. Find a pleasant and functional meeting place. Maybe the room should even be outside the building for a change of pace. Or, maybe the meeting should be held online (a "virtual" meeting").

Take a short course in conducting meetings. The key elements are known: start the meeting on time even if key people are missing, control time during the meeting, handle the overly vocal person and the quiet person, discourage side discussions, and keep the discussion rigid to the agenda. Some companies even hold stand-up rather than sit-down meetings, for example, at one unit of Sears Roebuck briefing meetings are stand-up.

Make provisions for recording results from the meeting. Appoint a scribe (before the meeting) and record key conclusions on a flip chart for all to see.

Consider the use of a facilitator. For cross-functional project team meetings, a facilitator is invaluable. The main roles are to assist the team leader to solve human relations problems among team members, provide training, revitalize a stalled project, and help in team building.

Close the huddle and get on to the next play. Give a quick summary of agreements and a list of action items with names and dates and a date and time for the next meeting if necessary. Ask attendees how the meeting could have been improved. And . . . end the meeting on time.

Follow-up after the meeting. At a minimum, provide a written summary of the meeting within 24 hours, either on a Web page or internal mail.

A useful website for conducting meetings – www.effectivemeetings.com – contains articles, checklists, and even shows how to calculate the cost of meetings. Another website shows managers how to facilitate real-time (multilocation) and Internet meetings. This latter website is www.technography.com.

MANAGING INFORMATION

In managing a department, we receive information by e-mail, Internet, fax, or regular mail. Some say that we are overwhelmed with information from many sources that is connecting us too much and causing work overload ("hyper connectivity").

Artificial intelligence techniques may someday provide us with a "personal assistant" to help us read and select information we receive through the computer. Meanwhile, today we must somehow do this ourselves or have an assistant do it. You can never read it all, so start by stopping some of the information you receive:

- Review internal material received (including e-mail), identify what you will not read, and eliminate your name from the distribution list.

- Drop subscriptions of business journals that you just place on a shelf and never read. For a change of pace, visit a library once a month to review journals and make copies of useful articles. Or subscribe to newsletters that select and summarize important articles in your field.

- Review how you handle e-mails. Most of us start the day by reviewing the new e-mails. This may be wrong because responding to e-mails detours us from the top priorities. The better approach would be to start the day by first reviewing the current written priorities and tentatively planning the day. Then look at the e-mails and decide how and when they will be handled. Some people read and answer e-mails at the end of the day. This helps to focus on the important ones and keep your responses short. Of course, setting priorities also applies to e-mails. These can be added to an A, B, C list of priorities based on the urgency, author of the e-mail, and other matters. Yes, some of these e-mails may never receive a response. Some managers provide selected people with a special e-mail address for truly urgent matters.

Guernsey (2001) reports that 39 percent of e-mail users have two e-mail accounts and 10 percent have five or more accounts. Rogen International, an Australian consultancy, reports that their 2001 survey revealed that executives spent at least two hours a day on e-mail. At one company, once a manager reaches a certain level, he is required to check (and respond to) his e-mail three times per day . . . 365 days per year. Technology speeds up our communication, but it usually does not speed up the analysis of the information in the e-mails.

In managing a department, a manager must first eliminate information that is not useful. But the manager must also collect information needed to run the department – including measures on work overload. For middle managers in operations, this means creating an information system that regularly reports performance data on the key processes for which the manager is responsible.

Some suggestions on selecting data to be collected:

1. Emphasize customer-related measurements – both internal and external customers.

2. Focus on measurements that are useful, not just easy to collect.

3. Provide for making measurements as close as possible to the activities they impact. This facilitates decision making and diagnosis when problems arise.

4. Provide not only concurrent indicators of performance but also leading and lagging indicators. Current and historical measurements are necessary, but leading indicators help to look into the future and prevent problems before they arise.

5. Emphasize measures that turn knowledge into action. Measures should directly link to operational goals or to

factors that contribute to meeting those goals. Pfeffer and Sutton (2000) develop a strong case for turning knowledge into action.

6. Periodically review the data collected and decide to continue, revise, or delete it.

Of course, data related to work overload should be a part of this system. Such data could include mandatory and voluntary overtime, personnel turnover, and other measures.

BUSINESS TRAVEL

Sometimes, the only effective way for people to exchange ideas and information is by a face-to-face meeting – and that often requires travel. Travel time certainly adds to work overload. But technology provides some fascinating alternatives that can help in our struggle to reduce work overload. These include:

- Videoconferencing. This is live, interactive video and audio communication among people at different locations. Thus, a typical business meeting could be held as a videoconference. My first experience, in 1985, was a revelation. A colleague and I appeared at a rented videoconferencing facility in New York City and spoke with a group of people in San Francisco. The two-hour conference was great – standard visual aids, a chalkboard, no special preparation, and no cross-country trip. A variation of a full videoconference consists of having a camera on top of a personal computer for video transmission and receipt.

- Web conferencing (also called net conferencing or web link). This uses computer file-sharing systems so that users can collaborate on graphics, slides, and speadsheets while linked by telephone. New computer files can be added throughout the discussion. Web conferencing is less expensive than video conferencing.

- Satellite broadcasting. This is a live broadcast by one person or a group of people, usually at one location, who beam a message to a large group of people at many locations. For example, a message from management to employees or customers could be delivered by satellite. The broadcast is one way but we can transmit questions or comments by phone to the broadcasting parties and provide a response to the satellite audience.

- Teleconference calls. This allows a number of people in different locations to talk live by phone.

- E-mail. This is excellent for exchange of basic information.

Any of these approaches lose some of the personal interaction of a face-to-face meeting, and sometimes that full interaction is essential. But these technological marvels can help to reduce work overload by reducing the amount of business travel (see Harmon 2000).

WHO ARE INDIVIDUAL PROFESSIONAL CONTRIBUTORS?

Individual professional contributors furnish the technical expertise to create, maintain, and improve the products and services of organizations. They have extensive formal education but usually do not have people reporting to them. Examples include physicians, nurses, teachers, social workers, accountants, and the many specialists in research and development, information technology, marketing, operations, and customer service. These people are strongly dedicated to their profession and often voluntarily have work overload. Tim Eitel, senior vice president of Raymond James, reminds us that some individual contributors are so wrapped up in their work that sometimes they need to be forced to back away from their work. The number-one concern of many professionals is trying to balance work and family demands.

A subset of individual professional contributors deserves mention. These contributors work in jobs with special characteristics:

- Continuous customer contact – all day long

- High volume of transactions

- Provide a critical (medical) service

- Service that often requires making mental judgments

- High degree of education and skills

- Interaction with co-workers, often involving the need to persuade others on a course of action

- Other

Examples of these positions are physicians, nurses, air traffic controllers, and traders on the stock market floor.

Professional contributors spend most of their time in the following activities:

- Scheduled appointments with customers

- Response to ad hoc customer requests

- Assigned projects

- Firefighting

- Professional learning

- Training other employees

- Meetings

- Business travel

- Volunteer service to professional societies

- Volunteer service to community organizations

Most individual contributors are not able to reduce their work overload. They don't have the time to analyze processes for waste; they don't have the interest in doing process analysis; and they don't have the skills to make the point effectively to middle and upper management. Therefore, nothing happens about work overload until the situation gets so bad that personnel leave the organization, serious errors are made, or other events occur that gain the attention of upper management. Then management may throw money and people at the overload problem without really studying the causes.

The working rules cited in Chapters 4, 5, and 6 for redesigning work content and redesigning for mental demands apply to this important subset of individual professional contributors.

OVERLOAD IN THE PERSONAL LIVES OF MIDDLE MANAGERS AND PROFESSIONAL CONTRIBUTORS

Actions to Minimize Work Overload

The aforementioned issues provide guidance to middle managers in minimizing and preventing work overload in their department. In addition, we can suggest some points that will help the middle manager minimize work overload in his or her own personal life. These include:

- Decide where you want to go in life and make plans to get there. These are long-range objectives for you and your family. This includes career objectives but also objectives for your family achieving a host of personal objectives – but based on a realistic assumption of financial resources. Don't let unrealistic personal desires drive you into work overload to achieve the financial resources needed to support the unrealistic desires. Good luck.

- Don't forget "essentials": exercise, sleep, spiritual, take time to do nothing. Also, practice relaxation and meditation techniques (see later in this chapter).

- Set long-range and short-range work objectives on what you want to accomplish. But be prepared to change those objectives, particularly the short-range objectives. Set weekly and daily objectives to: 1) keep a focus on the truly important tasks, and 2) alert you that your objectives for even a single day are too optimistic. Don't be concerned about not meeting those objectives – probably you will miss many of them. But learn from missing those objectives by realizing that you typically underestimate the time required to do many tasks. Of course, you may also learn that you have wasted time in many ways (a good lesson to learn) but equally important you may simply not be allowing enough time to do certain tasks. By having explicit goals and objectives, and not meeting them, it forces you to rethink the planning and scheduling of your work. Many people object that setting even informal objectives cannot be done because "there are too many variables – too many unexpected events that arise." My experience suggests that this is exactly when you need objectives so you can learn from operating in that environment of the unexpected. Two useful references on handling your work activities are St. James (2001) and Hutchings (2002).

- Avoid "hurry sickness," that is, the progressive need for task completion. Bruce A. Baldwin, a psychologist, aptly points out that some of us so enjoy the sense of getting a task done that we forget that delays are a part of life and that we should try to enjoy the doing of the job rather than fret at the delays to completing the task. This works fine if we are matched properly to a job and we truly enjoy what we are doing (see Chapter 7).

Checklists of actions are repeated in condensed form in the Appendix.

CARE AND WELL BEING OF MIDDLE MANAGERS AND PROFESSIONAL CONTRIBUTORS – LESSONS FROM ATHLETES

In many companies, work overload is not a serious issue. Congratulations to these companies. But other companies hire an inadequate managerial staff and workforce and then work everyone to the maximum.

When work overload exists, middle managers bear the brunt of the burden. The workforce understandably says, "I just work my eight hours and leave. If the work doesn't get done, that's my manager's problem." If there is an overload problem at the workforce level, a union can bring the problem to the attention of upper management.

Middle managers are responsible for meeting performance goals but fear bringing their personal work overload problem to the attention of upper management (middle managers do not have a union to act on their behalf). So upper management may not be aware of a work overload problem faced by middle managers. A doozie of a bad situation.

We start with a basic point: A middle manager is responsible to himself or herself and the family; the responsibility is not to the organization. Having said that, we realize that family responsibilities often focus around providing sufficient income to have a desired standard of living. This may mean both spouses working (perhaps with work overload for one or both spouses) complicated by overload on family activities because of the limited time available by the parents. One or both spouses may then accept a work overload problem in order to earn the income to "put food on the table." We will address this heavyweight situation in Chapter 11.

This book proclaims that the focus on work overload should be to redesign the job rather than teach the individual how to handle the stresses from work overload. But job redesign and other organizational changes will probably never eliminate work overload. Thus, we need to recognize the value of stress management concepts.

Much literature exists on how individuals should handle pressure and stress in the business environment. Psychologists base one approach that middle managers may like on research with world-class athletes. The result is a performance management model that addresses the body, the emotions, the mind, and the spirit, and I will use this model as a framework (see Loehr and Schwartz 2001). Another useful reference is *Mind and Body Medicine* (2001), a special health report from Harvard Health Publications (let's call it the MBM report). My following recommendations integrate those of the MBM report with the framework of the Loehr and Schwartz paper. For an excellent expansion of these concepts based on the research of a Harvard physician, see Benson and Proctor (2003). These references are authoritative, practical, and aimed at the layman.

The basic framework has four levels: physical capacity, emotional capacity, mental capacity, and finally, spiritual capacity (see Figure 9.1, Loehr and Schwartz 2001).

Each level influences the others, for example, exercise can produce a sense of emotional well-being, clearing the way for peak mental performance, leading to the idyllic spiritual purpose. This certainly sounds theoretical until we translate it into operational terms.

Physical Capacity

The key elements here are: at least seven hours of sleep, a proper diet for weight control, and exercise. Adding a 15-minute power nap is ideal. (Of course, don't eat lunch at your desk. A recent study of managers showed that 68 percent eat lunch at their desk at least once per week). Clearly, these elements are essential and difficult to

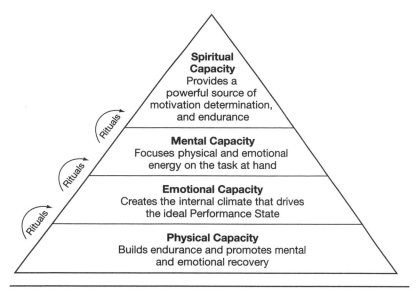

Figure 9.1 The high performance pyramid.

achieve but they are a MUST. Period. Much literature is available to help you.

The MBM report also suggests yoga (a combination of breathing exercises, meditation, stretch exercise, and strength exercise) and tai chi (a form of meditation).

Taking care of physical well-being is necessary . . . but not sufficient, so we move on to the next element.

Emotional Capacity

The key elements here are: identifying negative emotions and replacing them with positive responses. Again, this is difficult, but there are ways to manage the response to negative emotions.

The MBM report identifies 10 patterns of negative thinking:

- Exaggerating the importance of your mistakes

- Judging yourself based on complete success or complete failure (black-and-white thinking)

- Focusing on minor negative problems

- Assuming the worst will happen

- Discounting the positive as a fluke

- Labeling yourself negatively

- Drawing negative conclusions

- Allowing emotions to rule

- Applying rigid rules to yourself and others

- Blaming yourself for some negative event that was not your fault

Identifying these "personal cognitive distortions" (cognitive means mental) early alerts you to manage these in some way to prevent the stress from occurring. Various forms of relaxation techniques may be helpful. The MBM report suggests such approaches as meditation, progressive muscle relaxation, belly breathing, guided imagery (to imagine a calm scene), self-hypnosis, and even biofeedback.

Physical well-being and emotional capacity are both necessary but not sufficient, so we move on to the next element.

Mental Capacity

The key elements here are: focus, time management, and positive and critical thinking.

Maintaining focus means concentrating our energy to achieve a particular goal. Simple forms of meditation can be useful, for example, doing deep breathing exercises for 15 minutes in a quiet room.

Time management here does not refer to the techniques for distributing your efforts in the most efficient ways, but rather changing work routines to provide a more balanced view of life, for example, starting the day with jogging or swimming or some other exercise. Yes, that takes time but a benefit is both a higher-quality mental process and better physical capacity.

Positive and critical thinking help to generate optimism and well-being. Thinking occurs using some vehicle such as language, mathematics, and sensory skills such as sight and hearing. But another approach is visual imagery, for example, a golf ball rolling into the hole before a shot, or thinking about the desired outcome in a meeting about to take place.

Mental capacity is also necessary but not sufficient, so we move on to the last element.

Spiritual Capacity

The key element here is: use your deepest values to define a strong sense of purpose.

The MBM report suggests two approaches: social support and spirituality. Social support refers to social interaction with others, that is, marriage, co-workers, support groups, community groups. Doing an unexpected favor for someone can have quite an uplifting effect. Of course, you "don't have time," but then . . . make the time. You will be surprised if you do this when you are stressed and "don't have time." The positive reaction of the recipient of the favor will please you, relieve the stress, and convince you that it's important to find time to do it often.

In spirituality, we use prayer to induce a meditative state that encourages relaxation. The workplace is seeing a spiritual revival – not enormous but small and growing. In the past, the mention of God in the business world would be unthinkable. Now, a small group of courageous executives are stepping forward to ask how they can address individual worker and societal issues – and still generate a profit. Some of the companies who are active in these efforts include ServiceMaster, Blistex, Greyston Bakery, and Catalytica Pharmaceuticals. The executives are Christian and Jewish. An article that describes how some executives are applying the concept is "God and Business," by Marc Gunther (2001). Another useful reference is *The Power of Positive Thinking in Business*, by Scott Ventrella (2001). Ventrella was formerly on the staff of the Peale Center. Dr. Peale was the author of the famous book *The Power of Positive Thinking*. Ventrella discusses 10 traits of a positive thinker in business: optimism, enthusiasm, belief, integrity, courage, confidence, determination, patience, calmness, and focus. Ventrella's website is www.positivedynamics.com.

Rituals and Rejuvenation

A practical technique can help translate these concepts into action. The research with athletes discovered the need for "recovery" events every 90 to 120 minutes. The recovery is an event that is a change of pace and permits the body – and mind – to replace the energy (physical and mental) expended. These "rituals" might include some favorite music, a walk to the water cooler, a brief chat with a colleague, a 10-minute stop at a park or a place of worship on the way home from work, writing some pleasant events in a diary, thinking of a favorite joke, or looking at a door and imagining that someone you love walks in. A few courageous companies even have a room for taking a nap. One of my sons attends a weekly meeting where, for each meeting, a person is assigned to tell a joke at the beginning of the meeting. Now people get to the meeting on time . . . to hear the joke. You could start that in your organization tomorrow.

Athletes use rituals often, for example, examining the strings on a tennis racket in between sets, a baseball batter adjusting a glove between pitches. Other examples are dancing, gardening, petting an animal, or any event that helps you to unwind. Of course, you need to create rituals that work best for you – some you will do alone, some you may wish to do with others, whatever works. Dr. Clayton Long of The University of Tampa refers to these rituals as "rejuvenation time." He also observes that introverts use quiet time and extroverts benefit from social interaction as rituals.

Let's face it. If a person cannot recharge occasionally, he or she will not be mentally alert to perform strenuous mental tasks. Inevitably, they start to cut corners on their work ("it's good enough"), and this leads to errors and omissions that then require rework time resulting in work overload.

The Gilbreths and other early industrial engineers provide an analogy. Most factory jobs involved physical strength and endurance. When a job was timed, a fatigue allowance was added to the basic time for the job to reflect that the physical body needed some time to recover from the physical stresses acquired from doing the work. Depending on the degree of physical effort, the allowance might be 15 percent added to the basic time required to complete one cycle of the job. Today, machinery handles many (not all by any means) of the physically strenuous jobs. But many of these physical jobs have been replaced by jobs requiring mental and emotional traits that can lead to stresses. Thus, we need to think about an allowance for this and, therefore, the concept of rituals for recovery.

If you want to score yourself on stress, Hutchings (2002) provides questions for three types of stress: situational (major life events), physical, and emotional.

HOW LONG DOES IT TAKE FOR STRESS MANAGEMENT TO WORK?

Stress management does work, but there is a price to pay. That price is an investment of about 12 continuous weeks of sustained practice before the full effect takes place. After about six weeks, the effect will be noticeable and encourage you to continue. After 12 weeks, most people are hooked on the activities and will do their best to continue. People who have work overload "don't have the time" to do sustained practice. But, if they make that investment of 12 weeks they will become addicted – yes, addicted – and will make the time. That's why my friend, Bob Williams, is in the community swimming pool at 5:30 a.m. four days a week. Try.

CAN'T WE ACT ON WORK OVERLOAD TOMORROW?

Yes. This book recommends that the primary thrust to reduce work overload must be to eliminate waste from processes and redesign individual jobs to reduce excessive mental demands. That won't happen overnight. In Chapter 10, we will provide guidance on how to convince upper management to act. And that won't happen overnight. Meanwhile, you may have people (including yourself) who need help tomorrow.

What can we do? Here's a lineup of potential plays in this predicament:

1. Eliminate mandatory overtime (to force the study of waste in processes).

2. Set a target date for eliminating the work overload.

3. Set up an employee roundtable to brainstorm ideas on how to ease the overload.

4. Hire temporary help.

5. Request "shared resources" temporarily from another department.

6. Give a person who just finished a high overload project a new temporary project that he or she personally enjoys, to partially overcome the suffering from the overload.

7. Identify and reduce excessive mental demands in key jobs.

8. Provide compensatory time off.

9. Add fun to the work.

10. Encourage people to do recovery/rejuvenation rituals every 90 to 120 minutes.

11. Pull out the stops on reward and recognition.

Can you do all of these? Of course not, but several base hits can score some runs. This list is repeated in the Appendix.

SUMMARY – THREE KEY POINTS

1. Middle managers are the backbone of an organization, but they suffer from work overload because people come at them from both above and below.

2. To reduce work overload, middle managers must take short-term actions on their own activities but also long-term actions to convince upper management to address work overload as a broader problem.

3. Individual professional contributors provide the technical expertise for an organization, but many also suffer from work overload. Professionals in healthcare, air traffic control, investment transactions, and other areas could write a book on work overload.

What's missing from all this? The leadership of upper management – the next chapter.

10

What Is the Role of Upper Management in Work Overload?

Joe and Dennis are upper managers in two companies. Joe is always learning from others – even though he has a casual brilliance. He assembles the right team of smart people, delegates, stays out of the way, but is there to help when needed. Wow, does he communicate – not just "walking around," but using the latest technologies to keep all levels informed. He encourages openness at all times; he wants to hear the good and the bad. His ethics rest on one principle: do the right thing. He is deliberate and calm and looks like he is about to milk a cow. Dennis manages by fear and intimidation ("I'm the boss"). Push, push, push, if people can't handle it they can be replaced. He is a micromanager, frequently interfering in activities to inject his "better ideas." It's clear to all that if you bring Dennis bad news, you will be criticized in the presence of your peers. Ethics? To Dennis, the truth is negotiable. Dennis is intense and looks like he is about to bark.

Upper managers fall in between these two extremes.

MY PERCEPTIONS ABOUT UPPER MANAGEMENT

Upper management strives to satisfy numerous – and sometimes conflicting – demands of customers, employees, regulatory agencies, shareholders, and a board of directors. All of this in a highly competitive marketplace. Frankly, few people have the capability to be successful upper managers. It's a tough job, and anyone who thinks otherwise has not worked closely with upper management.

We ask upper management for leadership on so many parameters – profit, ethics, community affairs, product quality, diversity of employees. Now we ask for their leadership on work overload. Enlightened upper managers realize that work overload of their people can be a serious problem that must be addressed, solved, and prevented in the future.

But those upper managers who manage by fear and intimidation justify their actions as necessary to meet competition from other companies. Many of these managers are successful – at least in the short run. For these managers, work overload of employees is not a major problem, "it's a fact of business life."

Upper managers suffer from many of the same problems as middle managers. A question was posed to 1400 CFO's: What is greatest challenge for financial executives today? The results: 36 percent said time management; 27 percent said keeping up with technology; 19 percent said achieving work/life balance; 13 percent said staying current with accounting regulations. (See *USA Today*, 2001).

Most upper managers work long hours, are engrossed in their work, and simply do what's necessary to get the job done. Many of these managers clearly have work overload. But they don't understand that the rest of us are mere mortals and their employees view that work overload differently. When upper managers pile the work on employees, those employees view the manager actions as disrespectful.

Chapter 9 provides some short-term actions on work overload. But work overload is a complex problem that often requires a strategy to solve the problem. The approach involves two steps: 1) convince upper management of the seriousness of the problem, and 2) develop and implement a strategy to reduce and control work overload. We discuss these next.

HOW TO CONVINCE UPPER MANAGEMENT THAT WORK OVERLOAD IS A SERIOUS PROBLEM

Can we convince upper management to take action on work overload? The answer is"yes." But (you knew there would be a but) we need to rustle up a convincing case.

Sometimes upper management is simply not aware that a work overload problem exists. This can happen when:

- Labor budgets are tight and managers are discouraged from adding people, that is, managers are encouraged to run a "lean" operation.

- Skilled labor is scarce and it is difficult to fill open personnel requisitions.

- Middle management is fearful to bring the problem to upper management because it indicates that middle management cannot properly manage the department.

- Upper management (and middle management) does not realize that key processes have much waste and that this is a contributing cause of work overload. Therefore, they simply live with the problem and hope that they don't lose key people because of work overload.

- Other reasons.

Middle managers often say, "The overload problem should be obvious to upper management but they don't care about overload and therefore take no action." The realities are: 1) upper management loses touch with employees two or more levels below, and 2) upper management accepts work overload as part of their job and is complacent about the feelings of the rest of the organization.

We all know that "people resist change." That includes some upper management people. To quote the American economist John Kenneth Galbraith: "Faced with a choice between changing one's mind and proving that there is no need to do so, almost everybody gets busy on the proof."

In my experience, when upper management becomes aware of a problem, most of them first try to understand the nature and seriousness of the problem. If upper management makes a judgment that the problem requires action they ask for proposals, evaluate the proposals, and then makes decisions. Of course, all of this must be done within the constraints of cost and time.

Upper management is confronted with many problems and must make difficult decisions often based on the impact of problems on cost, and we cannot expect them to take action on work overload unless we present them with a compelling case to change the status quo on work overload. It is the responsibility of middle management to make that compelling case. In the steps that follow, watch for opportunities to get upper management personally involved in the process by encouraging them to offer ideas for any of the steps. In the first step, we find out the size of the problem.

FIND OUT THE EXTENT OF WORK OVERLOAD

Frankly, nothing will happen on work overload until upper management is convinced of the seriousness of the problem. Then how will we convince them? By presenting them with facts on work overload, stated in the language of upper management, that is, costs and sales revenue. We need to assemble data that shows, in dollars, how much money the organization is losing (yes, losing) each year due to work overload.

We can show what work overload costs an organization each year. The main elements are shown in Table 10.1.

Table 10.1 Costs of work overload.

- Extra costs
  - Mandatory overtime
  - Voluntary overtime
  - Lost sales income from potential customers due to inferior output
  - Lost sales income due to defections of current customers caused by inferior output
  - Cost of correcting inferior output
  - Cost of lower productivity during overload hours
  - Cost of scrap
  - Cost of downgrading product
  - Cost of excessive inspection to find inferior output
  - Cost of investigating and settling complaints on inferior product

---

continued

---

continued

    – Product warranty charges due to inferior product
    – Worker compensation costs and extra insurance costs
  • Personnel resignations
    – Resignations of key employees, as revealed in exit interviews
    – Recruiting and retraining costs due to resignations

Sometimes, just collecting the costs of work overload is sufficient to spur management action.

Some of these costs can be obtained from established operating records, but some other costs must be estimates. To establish credibility for the data, obtain the estimates from sources that have responsibility for the data, for example, accounting, marketing, human resources, and quality.

Additional steps could include:

• Have the accounting department assemble data on unexpended vacation time for middle managers and individual professional contributors.

• Have the human resources department conduct an audit of departments to determine the extent of work overload for both managers and the workforce.

• Consider the impact of work overload on families. This may have an impact on upper management as they can relate that situation to their own family life.

• Ask upper and middle management what other information should be collected in order to understand the size and nature of the overload.

• Consider bringing in an outside consultant to study the extent of work overload and propose further analysis and action.

Knowing the size of the problem, we can analyze the data to prepare a case for upper management.

ANALYSIS OF THE OVERLOAD DATA

Now the hard work begins. The data analysis and subsequent discussions must focus on a theme of upper management helping middle management to solve the overload problem. Simultaneously, middle management must realize that the overload problem will need to be solved in steps. Patience and cooperation must be the by words.

Sometimes, upper management "throws people at a problem" to show dramatic action (and not spend any more time discussing the problem) But if adding people to solve an overload in one area means reassigning people from other areas, this results in work overload in the areas where resources are "borrowed" – particularly if there is an "add-on" effect.

The analysis and discussion of the data can proceed in several ways:

- Have the upper management leadership team (current jargon for the top person and the direct reports) discuss the data at a regular top management meeting. But make sure work overload is an early agenda item so there is sufficient time for discussion. The discussion will probably require several regular meetings.

- Set up a task force of several members of the leadership team to analyze the data and present recommendations to the full upper management leadership team.

- If initial analysis shows that the overload problem is concentrated in one or several departments, the department heads can analyze the data and meet with upper management to present recommendations to relieve the overload.

For complex situations of work overload, it may be necessary to break up the total problem into parts and use a project team (see Chapter 8) for each part. An upper management task force could define the parts and define the mission of each project team. The human resources department could facilitate the project teams and coordinate the total effort.

Whatever approach is taken, upper management must lead the discussion to emphasize a priority in reducing overload, give necessary approvals to action, and set up mechanisms to follow through to assure that the problem is solved and steps taken to prevent future work overload.

CONVINCING UPPER MANAGEMENT TO ACT ON WORK OVERLOAD

Convincing upper management to take action on an important issue is, to use an old-fashioned word, tough. Upper management is presented with many proposals on a wide variety of issues. Many of these proposals are worthwhile but often require resources that are never in sufficient quantity to honor all proposals. Proposals to reduce work overload are particularly sensitive. My viewpoint is that proposals to reduce work overload are in competition with other proposals. We must present upper management with a solid case to act on work overload.

My suggestions on building that solid case are summarized in Table 10.2.

Table 10.2 Elements to justify action on work overload.

Focus on upper management priorities
- Tie in to overall company strategies
- Tie in to personal priorities of upper management

Quantify the seriousness of work overload problem
- Data on extra costs due to work overload
- Data on personnel resignations
- Personal observation by upper management

Gain the support of others
- Individual support of other functions
- Team of middle managers to study work overload

Create a proposal
- No surprises
- Benchmark against other organizations
- Present alternative solutions
- Watch the timing

Focus on Upper Management Priorities

Building such a case should show how a strategy to reduce work overload contributes to higher-level priorities to improve and sustain overall organization effectiveness.

Find out (from upper management confidants) the current priorities of upper management and try to address these priorities (not yours) in presenting a strategy to reduce work overload. Addressing the "bottom line" by estimating the cost of work overload may carry the day, but other factors such as reducing labor turnover and building trust with employees may be current priorities and actions to reduce work overload could produce tangible results to help these other priorities.

Quantify the Seriousness of the Work Overload Problem

Data can be collected to quantify the extra costs incurred due to work overload. Examples of such costs are listed in Table 10.1.

Data can be collected to quantify the impact of work overload on employee retention and resignations. Again, see Table 10.1.

Sometimes, the simple act of observation by upper management can help. Judith Lyons of Vista Plan Solutions reminds us that "the best senior managers start the day by walking through operations and they repeat the walk in the afternoon because the pace picks up." Observing what work overload means in practice can be persuasive.

Gain the Support of Others

If you have responsibility for operations, try to gain the support of other functions that are affected by inferior output from operations due to work overload. These functions might include marketing, human resources, customer service, and quality.

Propose that a middle manager team be created to study work overload. This brings new inputs on the seriousness of the problem and possible solutions. From all of this a consensus can emerge to present to upper management.

Create a Proposal

No surprises. None of us like surprises that put a roadblock in some plans that we have. Upper management is no exception. The first time that upper management hears about a serious work overload problem should not be when a formal proposal is made to take action.

Find out what other organizations are doing about work overload. This benchmarking not only provides additional ideas but also provides evidence that effective action can be taken. Upper management talking with their counterparts at other organizations can really be persuasive.

Several alternative actions (with the pros and cons) to reduce work overload can be useful. Presenting only one action may ignite some negative reaction from upper management and invite outright rejection of the proposal. Present several alternatives to provide upper management with actions that meet their priorities. Consider proposing that a consultant be brought in to study work overload.

Change can come at right and wrong times. Choose the right time. But keep the discussion going without pushing for immediate agreement. Look for, and present, additional information that will help promote agreement at a later time

Kolb and Williams (2001) provide valuable ideas on negotiating to achieve agreement on any issue.

ISSUES FOR UPPER MANAGEMENT TO CONSIDER ON WORK OVERLOAD

As upper management deliberates on work overload, some issues will emerge:

- Many CEO's have boundless energy. Workaholic managers, starting at the top, expect their people to be workaholics – and this is simply wrong. It's just a question of time before their people leave.

- Upper management must evaluate the impact of downsizing and/or mergers on work overload. These dramatic events often achieve financial savings by reducing personnel. Uncertainty about jobs coupled with an already existing level of work overload can be a disaster, particularly during the transition period. Finally, those remaining in the organization often find themselves doing more work, that is, work overload.

- Make priorities crystal clear so managers can allocate resources to the sequence of priorities. For 2004, the National Enterprise Operations Division of Bank One states the top priorities as "Partner of Choice" (Percent Shared Objectives Met), "High Performance Culture" (Percent Employee Engagement), "Financial Discipline" (Percent Unit Cost Met), and "Industry Leadership" (Percent Services in Top Tier). These priorities are established and communicated via their Commitment Flowdown™ (the Commitment

Flowdown™ is a proprietary methodology of Orion Advisory, LLC, www.OrionAdvisory.Com).

- Work overload has a large impact on the personal and family life of employees, and upper management needs to accept some responsibility for this.

- Work overload, if not corrected, causes high labor turnover resulting in extra costs, poor quality delivered to customers, and poor delivery response to customers.

- Management style and practices contribute to work overload. No one respects a manager who manages by fear and intimidation or a manager who repeatedly becomes involved in activities at lower levels (micromanaging) instead of setting directions and providing support. Examples of poor management practices (see Chapter 5) include lack of management support, lack of career planning, and lack of family-friendly practices. When these practices combine with work overload, employees are not just tired but they are mentally and emotionally stressed leading to burnout (while the employee searches for a position in another company).

- When it is not possible to quickly relieve overload, management must at least show concern and empathy. A simple step is this: walk through operations every few days and stop to talk with people. My research on workforce teams spawned a story. A company held a banquet for those who had participated on teams. All appreciated the party, but one person remarked, "This was the first time I have ever seen the plant manager – too bad he doesn't walk through the shop once in a while." Why can't all upper managers be like Jamie Dimon, CEO of Bank One? He is a wizard in making connections with all levels at the bank.

- An organization needs to be careful that it is not trying to be "best" at too many different parameters, that is, cost, quality, product innovation.

> *Old Italian proverb: He who commences many things finishes but few.*

- Have human resources conduct exit interviews for those who choose to leave the company. Among other questions, ask "Was your workload reasonable and satisfactory to you?"

- The action plan on work overload must include: 1) steps to implement the action; 2) steps to assure that the action was successful in relieving work overload; and 3) measures to periodically track and/or audit work overload in the future.

Eventually, you will present a strategy for reducing work overload – but not before you have taken the aforementioned steps to convince management that the problem is serious. The discussion so far has focused on the seriousness of the problem. Next, we will focus on developing the strategy.

DEVELOPING A STRATEGY ON WORK OVERLOAD

A strategy on reducing work overload and preventing future work overload must answer four questions: 1) how will work overload be measured? 2) how much reduction in work overload is desired? 3) what approach will be taken to reduce the work overload? and 4) what specific principles and policies will be followed to reduce the current level of work overload and maintain the new level in the future? Here are the key steps in developing a strategy to reduce work overload:

1. Define the operational goals for your department. These might be:

   - Process X checks per day.

   - Meet a labor budget of $Y per month.

   - Meet an error rate of no more than Z processing errors per day.

   These goals do not address work overload (yet). The approach is to first convince upper management that you are starting with a bottom line perspective.

   You will also need to present data on how well these goals are being met (or not met).

2. Determine the current level of work overload and how this relates to bottom-line financial measures (see previous discussion on quantifying the cost of work overload). For example, the current work overload might be that 35 percent of the employees have been on mandatory overtime during the past three months and, if this level of overtime continues, it will result in an extra cost of $X,000 per year. Another measure of the cost of work overload could be data on retention of key employees. If work overload appears to have caused injuries that have increased insurance costs, then these extra costs can be quantified. This step is meant to convince upper management that work overload is serious and action must be taken.

3. Take steps to determine and remove the key causes of work overload. We have identified in Chapter 2 10 contributing causes of work overload. But you need to identify the key factors in *your* organization. One way to obtain this information is to use a written survey asking employees to review the 10 factors in Chapter 2 (or prepare your own list based on input from a sample of employees) and divide 100 points among the factors to indicate the relative importance. Caution: such a survey understandably raises the expectations of employees, that is, they expect to see changes made. Also, they will request (again, under-standably) a written summary of the results. Getting input of affected employees (not just their supervisors) should be a key part of the strategy. Do this as an early step.

   Also, a focus group of employees (guided by a facilitator) can be asked to discuss the factors contributing to work overload.

   In addition to these data on employee perceptions, other data can help to convince management. For example:

   - Various forms of waste in the processes. This waste uses human resources. Chapters 3, 4, and 5 described how to identify the waste and redesign the process and the individual jobs to eliminate the waste and reduce the work overload.

   - Unfilled personnel requisitions. Perhaps these average 16 each month or 11 percent of the personnel authorized. As a benchmark, a similar department in the XYZ Company averages about 4 percent.

- Computer software and hardware problems. Typically, the minimum number of problems is X per week (with an average of Y per week). These problems involve computer downtime resulting in work stoppages that later cause work overload to catch up to meet customer processing requirements. As a benchmark, a similar activity at the RTU Company averages about K per week.

- Work process not capable of meeting quantity or quality requirements. A recent random sample revealed that about 31 percent of people's time was spent on finding and correcting errors in the process. This extra time results in a work overload to meet customer requirements on processing. As a benchmark, the number at the GHJ Company is 12 percent. The reasons why a work process is not capable can involve work design, personnel selection and training, inputs from internal and external suppliers, and other reasons.

- Insufficient resources to handle a normal workload. Even if waste is eliminated from processes, the resources currently assigned may still not be sufficient. But this point must be proven to upper management by studying the capability of the process and providing data to show that current resources are not sufficient.

Note how this presentation (to management) makes use of two concepts: 1) a numerical value of the size of the critical factor, and 2) a comparison to a similar organization. It is agreed that it is not always possible to include one or both of these concepts, but they sure make the case stronger.

As you collect data on the factors contributing to work overload, watch for the "Pareto principle." This principle says that in any population that contributes to a common effect, a relative few of the contributors – the "vital few" – account for the bulk of the effect. Thus, we must identify the vital few contributors to work overload (based on data) and focus our effort initially on these factors to obtain the fastest result.

A formal project-by-project approach may be necessary to tackle the main issues in work overload. Each "project" is a work overload issue to be solved. This approach has three main steps:

1. Prove the need by presenting data on the seriousness of the overload problem (see previous discussion).

2. Identify specific projects. This involves obtaining nominations for projects, deciding priorities, selecting initial projects to demonstrate the approach, and writing a problem and mission statement for each project.

3. Organize project teams and implement the projects. Typically, each team has a leader, members, a secretary, and a facilitator. Carrying out each project involves:

   • Verifying the project need and mission

   • Diagnosing the causes

   • Providing a remedy and proving its effectiveness

   • Dealing with resistance to change

   • Instituting controls to hold the gains

The detailed steps in this approach have been proven extensively in the business world. See, for example, my book on *Quality Planning and Analysis*. How do we convince upper management to authorize such an approach if it is needed? By using the bottom-line financial measure discussed previously in step 2.

This project-by-project approach involves not just an operations department but is cross functional and probably involves human resources, information technology, and likely other departments.

4. Set goals, with time targets, on removing the causes. For example, a goal on overall work overload might be no employee in the department shall have work overload for a period of two continuous months. Goals on critical factors might be:

   • Unfulfilled personnel requisitions: reduce to 10 percent in six months

   • Overtime: reduce overtime by 25 percent within one month

- Computer software and hardware problems: reduce to 20 in six months

- Process rework: reduce to 8 percent in six months

Even if these goals must be somewhat arbitrary, they provide guidance for the next step. That is, developing plans to achieve these goals.

Examples of successful internal efforts in each of the areas should be presented to convince upper management that an approach has been developed that works and what is needed is for upper management to authorize a continuation of this approach with assigned responsibility and resources.

5. Develop and implement plans to achieve the goals. These plans should include some principles or policies that should be followed to *prevent* work overload. Examples might be:

   - All new jobs will be analyzed to be sure that sufficient time is allotted and that employees have sufficient resources and training to meet all job requirements.

   - All jobs will be filled with a careful match of employee skills and job requirements.

   - The use of beepers after work hours will be discouraged.

   - Checking e-mail messages after work hours will be discouraged.

   - All employees will take a lunch break and this break may not be taken at their work station.

   - A family-friendly attitude will be encouraged (see Chapter 11).

   - A senior management person must spend one full day every two months in an activity with work overload.

Each goal should have a person or function designated as having the primary responsibility for coordinating all efforts to achieve that goal. For example:

- Unfilled personnel requisitions: Primary responsibility will be the human resources department working in conjunction with the operations department.

- Computer problems: Primary responsibility will be the information technology department working in conjunction with the operations department.

- Process not capable problems: Primary responsibility will be the operations department working in conjunction with the quality department and specified internal and external suppliers to the operations department along with internal staff departments or external consultants.

Each case should specify a date by which a corrective-action plan is developed and implementation started. Don't forget to provide for some fun in the process to ease the agony of overload.

An alternative to this is to ask upper management to appoint a cross-functional task force to study the work overload problem. The taskforce should be given a one-page mission statement stating the scope of the task force effort and giving a date for reporting to management.

6. Review progress with periodic measurements and audits of current work overload areas. The measurements should be in the same units of measure as the goals (step 4). Measures should focus on turning knowledge of the process into action on work overload.

   Measurements can also be supplemented with physical audits of work activities that have serious work overload. These can be brief visits to the work area to provide supplementary detail useful for corrective action. These audits can be made by a quality department, which usually has people trained as auditors to provide an independent and objective review of activities.

7. Provide for a periodic review with upper management of progress toward goals. This provides the essential leadership of upper management to assure resolution of the work overload problem. These reviews with upper management must lay the groundwork for execution of plans. Thus, clarify what the follow through will be, who will do the what, when and how, what resources they will use, and when the next review will take place. Bossidy and Charan (2002) present many useful ideas on execution in the business world.

8. Set up controls to continuously manage work overload. The control sequence for work overload includes:

- Identify the contributors to work overload.

- Establish how you would measure each contributor.

- Establish a standard for each contributor.

- Measure actual performance.

- Compare actual performance to the standard.

- Take action on the difference.

But this control sequence should be established for *all* key characteristics of a process – not just work overload. This is the way to *manage the process*, that is, periodically measure the important performance parameters for the operational goals of the department (step 1), identify problems early, and take action. This helps to *prevent* work overload by avoiding the need to assign resources (by adding to the work load of already busy people) to correct a problem. The big assumption here is that the processes have been analyzed and waste removed so that the processes are capable of meeting their performance requirements. Note that this control sequence for all key process characteristics identifies potential problems early and helps to prevent firefighting – a key cause of work overload

A key step in all this is measurement. Some principles can help us to develop effective measurements for quality. The six guidelines for measurement (see Chapter 9 under Managing Information) are helpful in planning for measurement.

To summarize, in the previous pages we have presented ideas to: 1) convince upper management of the seriousness of the work overload problem, and 2) develop a strategy for reducing and controlling work overload.

Now you are ready to make a presentation to management. Rehearse the presentation before a few observers who play the role of upper management by asking you questions that upper management might ask. Also, recognize the time pressures on upper management and, therefore, be concise. No digressions from the point.

OPERATIONAL ACTIONS THAT UPPER MANAGEMENT MUST TAKE

Some-high level operational actions are needed:

- Upper management should make clear that the total working hours must be kept within reason.

- Examine the status of products offered and customers served. Suppose a company offers 1000 different products, but 300 of the products account for only 4 percent of the total volume of sales. Also, suppose the company serves 450 different customers, but 50 of these customers account for only 5 percent of the total sales volume. The question arises: should the company offer all 1000 products and serve all 450 customers? Further analysis is needed to recognize other factors, but if some products could be eliminated and/or some customers declined, the resources saved could reduce work overload.

- Processes that are overloaded probably contain significant waste that should be identified and eliminated (see Chapter 3). If necessary, upper management must provide additional resources to study the processes and identify and eliminate the waste. This alone may free up enough resources to solve the overload problem. But upper management must direct that savings from process redesign be used to reduce work overload – instead of to increase profit. Only top management involvement can assure that this will happen.

- Upper management should watch for opportunities to help middle management in the middle management work overload problem. Sometimes a brief intervention by upper management can remove obstacles that are causing work overload for middle managers. For example, middle managers deal with middle managers at a supplier to resolve problems. When an impasse occurs (causing work overload due to the problem) a phone call by upper management to the upper management of the supplier can often resolve the problem quickly. Of course, asking upper management to intercede can only happen occasionally, but some occasions are the right time.

- Upper management must make sure that middle management has sufficient time to periodically review priorities for their units and review activities for work overload.

- Middle managers should be supported to pursue the actions discussed in Chapter 5 concerning the mental demands of jobs of subordinates (lack of management support, career concerns, and lack of family-friendly practices). Upper managers must support the concept of matching people to the right jobs (see Chapter 7). Employees in jobs that do not suit their abilities and interests quickly become unhappy and stress builds up to combine with work overload to cause problems. On the other hand, employees suited for their jobs are satisfied in the job and can handle significant work overload (at least for awhile) because they are happily focused on their work and the results that the work achieves.

- Pursue the actions discussed in Chapter 7 concerning retention of key personnel (retention data, employee opinion surveys, and outside research).

- Upper managers must search for creative solutions to the work overload problem and tap the ideas of all personnel to identify these creative solutions. One example is flextime in which employees are allowed some flexibility in choosing their working hours (see Chapter 11). The flextime may not directly reduce work overload, but it relieves some of the personal stresses that when combined with work overload cause serious problems.

- When it is not possible to quickly reduce overload, management must provide relieving (palliative) actions such as special time off to cushion the overload (and prevent disaster) until the overload can be reduced. Palliative actions are helpful but don't fight a fire with a water pistol. Stronger actions are needed.

- Inject some fun activities to lighten the burdens.

Finally, there is one more essential role for upper management. An important reason for work overload of middle managers is the lack of cooperation and teamwork among middle managers themselves. Longenecker and Neubert (2000) did research with 204 managers from 16 large manufacturing and service firms. The research identifies the factors that prevent front-line management from working together (for example, personality conflicts, conflicting goals rewards based on individual performance). The research also identifies the problems created by front-line management not working well together (communication breakdowns, wasted resources and efforts, increased job-related stress, and workplace tension). But a key research result is what front-line management thought necessary to achieve cooperation.

The five recommendations were:

1. Develop consensus around a common vision and super-ordinate goals that focus on organizational outcomes.

2. Implement team-based performance measurement, feedback, and reward systems.

3. Ensure that top management demonstrates and fosters cooperation in word and deed.

4. Promote the use of team building, skill development, and team training as common practices in organizational life.

5. Facilitate front-line management team involvement in and ownership of decision processes and outcomes.

Note that these recommendations address issues raised on the mental demands of jobs in Chapter 5. But to implement such concepts clearly requires the initiative and leadership of upper management.

To sum up, an enlightened upper management will address work overload of employees because it's the right thing to do – not because there's a payoff. Upper managers are confident people – sometimes wrong, never in doubt. They can solve the work overload problem.

SUMMARY – THREE KEY POINTS

1. Enlightened upper managers realize that work overload can be a serious problem for their employees and that it must be addressed; other upper managers (the flinthearted) choose not to address work overload of their people.

2. It is the responsibility of middle managers to convince upper managers to take action on work overload.

3. If a middle manager uses the approaches suggested and fails to convince upper management to act on work overload, then the middle manager should . . . resign.

Work and family activities interact. Companies can help their people to meet both job and family responsibilities. The next chapter shows how some companies step up to the plate to help employees.

11

What Are Work and Family Issues in Overload?

Laura, the mother hen at a regional bank, worked long hours for many reasons. She aggressively requested to be cross-trained in almost every job function in her division – she enjoyed staying busy, and she really needed the extra money. Laura had a primary job function – to manage and report time-card information. But working about 50 hours per week wasn't enough.

Laura's sister was terminally ill with just months to live and a family to care for; she had a husband also in poor health who recently lost his job as a car salesman. Laura was the breadwinner for an entire family tree.

Laura always had time to work, and she always did the work of two people. She was burdened with the pain and anxiety of poor health of family members, and she carried the burden with a smile and attitude of hope. Working longer hours than anyone else, often 70-80 hours a week to make ends meet, and then off to the hospital to visit her ailing sister and then quickly home to care for her husband. Laura always delivered holiday candy to her chosen few co-workers and superiors. Laura had her reasons. . . .

WORK AND FAMILY LIFE – TIMES HAVE CHANGED

A few decades ago, jobs were separate from family life; today, jobs and family life strongly interact. For many people, the realities of work put dramatic burdens on family life. A PBS program reported that family time has decreased by 22 hours per week since 1970. The contributing factors are:

- Both spouses work in about 64 percent of married couples with children under the age of 18. About 55 percent of mothers with children younger than one year old are working, about 61 percent with children under six years of age, and 79 percent with children 6-17 years old. These data come from the U.S. Census Bureau and the U.S. Bureau of Labor Statistics.

- In 13 percent of American families, one spouse is working simultaneously at two jobs, according to Bond, Galinsky, and Sawnberg (1998). Reich (2001) reports that the Bureau of the Census survey on "Households by Type and Selected Characteristics" shows that single-parents head more than 30 percent of families.

- Many Americans work longer hours than in the past. Reich (2001) reports that Americans work 350 hours per year more than Europeans.

Other factors also become intrusive to family life:

- The 24/7 work week. Some companies operate functions on three shifts and middle managers are on call for all three shifts, thus 24 hours a day, seven days a week. Technology makes this possible and serving global markets accelerates the scenario. Middle managers often pay a price if they are responsible for overall operations.

- Modern communication devices result in both advantages and additional burdens to middle managers. The devices include home faxes, voice mail, e-mail, beepers, cell phones, and car phones. Messages must be answered, often when the managers are at home. Responding includes sharing the information with other colleagues and this takes more time.

- Long commutes to work.

- Extensive business travel.

- Other.

Americans work longer hours (and often with both spouses working) to have sufficient income to achieve and maintain a desired standard of living. For upper and middle income people, this results in the desire to "keep up with the Jones's." (As a song from Lone Star Cafe goes: "We've been so busy keeping up with the Jones' four car garage and we're still building on.") Lower income people just try to maintain a bare minimum standard of living.

What does all of this mean? Several realities emerge:

- We are never satisfied. We need additional possessions to maintain satisfaction. Our needs today become a routine expectation tomorrow particularly in light of what our friends possess.

- Organizations know how to discover "hidden customer needs" – the needs that customers have yet to discover. (My book *Quality Planning and Analysis* even discusses how companies can discover these needs). The organizations see the opportunities and they develop products to meet the needs. Some of these new products are highly beneficial; some of them are simply trivial gimmicks. The point is this: our desire for more and more products contributes to the need for additional income and this leads to work overload.

- We love to shop. In her thought-inspiring book *The Overworked American*, Juliet Schor (1992) states the case well: "Once purely a utilitarian chore. Shopping has been elevated to the status of a national passion. For some people, shopping has become an addiction, like alcohol or drugs." Blunt, but does the shoe fit?

- Marketing practices are persuasive – they create desire for new products and enable more people to purchase those products.

So, wonderful products emerge and societal forces create our desire, thus leading to the need for additional income. The result is a more intense pace of work life, that is, work overload.

But the pace of work life merges with the pace of family life to become a distressing combination.

THE PACE OF FAMILY LIFE

America has an enviable standard of living. (Unfortunately, we still have a wide gap between the "haves" and the "have nots.")

Part of that standard of living is a wonderful array of family activities – to those families who have the income and the time to afford these activities. Consider the athletic programs for children. Team sports are softball, baseball, hockey, soccer, basketball, football, swimming, and more. But think of the transportation involved (usually by the mothers), not just for the games but also for the many practices. In theory, participation can be limited to a few sports, but in real life, the participation in sports creates a burden for the family. A group of mothers in Minnesota reached two conclusions: 1) they were strongly in favor of the benefits of the sports programs, and 2) the time involved for all concerned was getting out of hand. Discussion with the coaches focused on what might be done to retain the programs but reduce the time involved. The parents even set up a website (www.familylife1st.org) to encourage other communities to try ideas.

Most of us do volunteer work at a school, a religious activity, a community organization – often in the evening. Some people attend a monthly meeting of their professional society, again in the evening.

Families even "outsource" some activities to save time. Examples are childcare, cleaning, food preparation, even dog walking. Thus, time is an issue and when one or both spouses work then overload at the workplace is further compounded by time overload in family activities. Some of the stories are humorous (but highlight a problem): a mother and father schedule a family meeting each week, all must be present, and no outside activities are permitted to interfere.

In addition to time overload, some activities require money such as golf, equipment for hockey and football, and horseback riding. These expenses add pressure to earn more income and this leads to more work overload. These comments apply to middle income people. Imagine the situation for low income people, for example, the wife who works as a housekeeper at a hotel during the day and her husband who works as a doorman during the evening. Lucky for them that their employer is Marriott, one of the leaders in work-family programs.

Is the answer to follow a life of "simplicity" – focus on the true needs for your existence? It's worth a try – start by reading some books on keeping life simple. But I agree with Robert Reich that it isn't easy to distinguish between "needs" and "wants." We don't live in a vacuum where we can decide what we need and restrict those needs to what we can afford. Instead, we live in a world with extended family, friends, a work community, and a social community. In addition, technology provides an unending supply of new products and services, and marketing makes them irresistible. These factors lead to wants that go beyond basic needs and cause us to work harder to gain the income required for these new wants.

These are weighty matters for families to consider and make their individual judgments. For those who wish to examine these serious matters in more detail, two references are useful. Reich (2001) describes how the changing national economy has resulted in ever-expanding opportunities for all of us but at the price of a more hectic life. For your family, Doherty and Carlson (2002) show specifics of how families with overscheduled kids can take steps to lead a more balanced life. Here's my point: the hectic pace of family life further intensifies the stress created by overload from a job.

WHAT ORGANIZATIONS ARE DOING TO HELP – SEVEN ACTIVITIES

Some organizations have a family-friendly working environment.

⚜ *Old German proverb: A good example is half a sermon.* ⚜

Table 11.1 shows seven work-family activities that companies employ to help families.

Table 11.1 Seven work-family activities.

1. Flexible work options
   a. Flexible work schedules
   b. Working at home
   c. Job sharing
   d. Part-time work with partial or full health benefits
2. Assistance in meeting childcare needs
3. Assistance in meeting eldercare needs
4. Assistance in relocation of employees
5. Availability of family and medical leaves
6. Assistance with physical and mental health needs
7. Assistance in other family matters

Next, we discuss these seven activities. The examples cited come from the rankings of the "100 Best Companies to Work For" in *Fortune* magazine.

1. **Flexible work options**

   a. Flexible work schedules ("flex-time"). This permits the employee to schedule work hours to make it easier to handle family responsibilities, such as getting children to and from school. Baxter Healthcare has about 2000 employees on a flexible schedule or working at home.

      At American Century Investments, a mutual fund and brokerage organization, more than half of the employees have a flexible work schedule. At First Tennessee Bank, 93 percent of the employees say they take time off from work when they think it's necessary.

      Work has a serious impact on many families. Maybe we need to restructure the work from the traditional 40 hours, five days a week to whatever structure is needed. Surveys show that employees would give up some salary (or salary increases) in order to have time off – that's how bad the hectic pace has become). Other employees would not give up salary for time off, but at least the choice would be available.

   b. Working at home ("flex-place"). Employees may work at home allowing them to care for children (or elderly parents). Telecommunications tools are often involved leading to the term "telecommuting."

   c. Job sharing. Hewlett-Packard permits job sharing, even for some managers. This requires trust in each other and much communication.

   d. Part-time work with partial or full health benefits, if desired by the employee. Starbucks provides medical, dental, and vision coverage to all workers, including part timers. Federal Express covers healthcare for most part timers.

   These examples of flexible work options are available in many organizations. Such arrangements depart from traditional work arrangements and require careful planning among employees and managers. To facilitate the process of change, Bank One uses a six-step process for an employee to request a flexible work option and for the manager to review the request. These steps are shown in Figure 11.1.

	Whose Responsibility	
	Employee	**Manager**
Step 1: Identify the schedule you want Select the type of flexible work option you want to request. Identify the proposed schedule.	✔	
Step 2: Think through your request Using the Employee Worksheet and/or checklists, identify how the schedule will sustain your performance and affect others. Surface issues and identify solutions. If applicable, identify telecommunicating/work-at-home issues. Identify how your results will be evaluated, how the schedule itself will be monitored.	✔	
Step 3: Propose the request to your manager Take time to prepare your discussion. Review and complete the Employee Worksheet, putting yourself in your manager's shoes and in your customers' shoes. Fill out Section A of the Proposal-to-Plan form. Next, meet with your manager and discuss your proposal. Listen to your manager's questions, concerns, and ideas.	✔	
Step 4: Review the proposal Listen to the employee's proposal. Use the checklists in Section B to review the request. Review Tips for Success. Surface concerns. Refer to the Common Concerns section in the Guide. Consider solutions.		✔
Step 5: Take action Decide to approve or deny the request. Contact your Human Resources Business Partner about special or unusual issues or to ask specific questions (for example, overtime, changes to benefits, and so on) and under-stand all telecommuting/work-at-home issues before approving a request. Communicate your decision and the business reasons to the employee. Designate a pilot period. Complete Section C of the Proposal-to-Plan form. Keep a copy of the Proposal-to-Plan form in the employee's desk file. Send a copy of all completed proposals (approved and not approved) to your Human Resources Business Partner. If employee status changes, complete the appropriate paperwork.		✔
Step 6: Make the new approved schedule work Appropriately communicate changes to customers, co-workers, and others. Periodically review performance results and monitor how the schedule itself is working. Determine if the new work schedule will continue beyond the pilot period.	✔	✔

Figure 11.1 Proposal-to-Plan process.

Flexible work options are often the main part of a company program. But other services are also a part of work-family programs. These include:

2. **Assistance in meeting childcare needs.** This includes on-site childcare facilities, financial assistance for off-site options, or financial assistance to communities to develop childcare facilities. PBS reports that good quality day care for two kids can cost as much as $1100 per month – that may be a quarter of a double income. But companies can help. MBNA America Bank provides affordable childcare at $119-$150 a week. Amgen Corp. has a childcare center for 450 children. AFLAC has a childcare center with a monthly rate of only $292. EMC not only has on-site childcare but also summer camp programs for children.

3. **Assistance in meeting eldercare needs.** Some workers must take time off, may lose out on preferred job assignments and promotions, retire early, or even resign because of the pressures of eldercare. A Met Life study of more than 1500 workers who provide eldercare revealed some sobering data, for example, 64 percent had to take sick days or vacation time, 22 percent needed a leave of absence, and 13 percent retired early. Eldercare responsibilities will escalate rapidly as the population gets older.

4. **Assistance in relocation of employees.** Eli Lilly realizes that relocation of employees raises significant problems for families. The company furnishes assistance in areas ranging from spousal employment, housing, and children's sports.

5. **Availability of family and medical leaves** – with or without salary. At the Edward Jones Company, a broker who has a baby is guaranteed 75 percent of her average commissions for six weeks after delivery. ACXIOM provides a week of paid leave for new fathers.
   The Family and Medical Leave Act of 1993 provides up to 12 weeks per year of unpaid leave for medical emergencies. Reich (2001) believes ultimately we must have paid family leave for emergencies (like most other countries). A few (about 5 percent) companies even offer leaves of absence with salary and benefits. The "sabbatical leaves" permit employees to engage in almost any activity to revitalize themselves and return to work with a new

lease on life. Among the companies are American Century, Charles Schwab, Frank Russell, Nike, and Time Inc. (Browning 2003).

6. **Assistance to help employees with physical and mental health needs.** MBNA America Bank supplies a 24-hour hotline for medical advice. Hallmark's Compassionate Connections program helps workers to deal with stress and grief.

7. **Assistance in other family matters such as retirement planning and adoption assistance.** MBNA America Bank donates up to $20,000 support for adoption, and additional services. Home Depot presents a financial education program on matters including developing budgets, understanding credit, and home buying. Marriott with 116,000 hourly employees has a hotline to help employees locate affordable day care, find apartments or homes, or a host of other issues. Bank One even has a "homework hotline" with a teacher to help students. Marriott also helps employees who have problems with the English language. Amgen Corp. has a weekly farmers market. These organizations provide creative approaches to helping families. Rose (2003) describes work-life initiatives in various companies including the impact on parameters such as job satisfaction and employee retention.

ELIMINATION OF MANDATORY OVERTIME

A 1997 study by the Families and Work Institute reports that nearly one in five employees is required to work paid or unpaid overtime once per week with little or no previous notice. Alternatives to mandatory overtime are available: make overtime voluntary, or substitute compensatory time off for overtime salary. Of course, the pressure for additional family income means that many people will want the overtime hours but . . . at least they will have a choice. Why must we eliminate mandatory overtime? Simply because it's the right thing to do. At the Vanguard Group of mutual funds, employees can even buy an extra week of vacation.

THE TOP COMPANIES ON WORK – FAMILY PROGRAMS

For companies to institute work-family practices requires a change in traditional thinking. The reasons why it can't be done are endless, but the impressive list of companies with work-family programs tells us that it *can* be done. *Working Mother* magazine (Oct. 2003) identified the 100 best companies for working mothers. Among the top 10 were (alphabetically): Abbott Laboratories, Booz Allen Hamilton, Bristol-Myers Squibb Co., Eli Lilly and Company, Fannie Mae, General Mills, IBM Corporation, Prudential Financial Inc., S. C. Johnson & Son, Inc., and Wachovia Corporation. My compliments to these 100 organizations. Let's hold them up as examples to the other organizations that simply offer excuses why it can't be done.

Baxter Healthcare believes that the key to business success is: have the right people. To get those top people, Baxter realizes the company must have flexibility in personnel practices. If a company really believes that getting the right people is paramount, then the company will overcome the obstacles to providing work-family practices.

Friedman and Greenhaus (2000) present the results of research based on survey data from about 860 employed alumni of two business schools. Their research examines "the effects of gender, professional culture, and social expectations on the evolving roles of men and women in crafting an integrated life."

BENEFITS OF WORK-FAMILY PROGRAMS

Organizations with strong work family programs report the following benefits:

- Improve employee satisfaction, which, in turn, leads to improved customer satisfaction. This applies to those having direct contact with customers and those who work behind the scenes.

- Recruit new employees with superior skills and experience. Increasingly, job candidates can choose among employers based not only on the position but also on work scheduling flexibility and other aspects of a job.

- Retain talented employees. The bottom-line savings are the time and cost saved to recruit, interview, and train a new hire. See Chapter 7 for some convincing data.

- Promote a balanced life for employees to enable them to achieve personal goals in family, education, and community activities.

- Enhance community relations because satisfied employees present a positive image of the company to the community.

An "Alliance of Work/Life Professionals" who work in business, academia, or the public sector aims to promote a healthy balance between work and personal life (their website is www.awlp.org).

HOW TO INSTITUTE WORK FAMILY PROGRAMS

First, how should we present the case to upper management? A good approach combines financial data with information on employee demographics and needs (discussed next, and information on the benefits of a program (discussed previously).

Lack of work-family programs results in absenteeism and employee turnover. These two factors can be quantified in dollars.

Information on employee demographics includes the number of working mothers, number of mothers with children in school, number of employees with eldercare responsibilities, number of employees who are recent immigrants and who may have problems with language or other matters, and other statistics. Sometimes, if we just collect these numbers and present them to management the impact can be surprising.

Next, we must determine what the employees need to balance their work life with their family life. How do we find out? Use employee surveys and small focus groups, run by a trained focus group facilitator.

Work-family programs do cost money. Some of the needed funds can come from increases in worker productivity. These increases in productivity should not come from making employees work faster and harder. They should come from eliminating waste in processes – a key focus of this book. If a company has a quality improvement or performance improvement program based on the project-by-project approach, then projects aimed at work overload can be identified and pursued by improvement teams.

As an industrial engineer I believe we should divide monetary savings from eliminating waste in five ways, in order of priority: 1) reduce work overload; 2) work-family programs for employees; 3) increases in salary and benefits to employees; 4) funds for additional productivity improvement efforts so that improvements become a way of life; and 5) distribution to shareholders – the people who endow the financial foundation for the company.

The next section of this chapter describes how Marriott developed and applied its program.

The Middle Manager and Work-Family Programs

The job flexibility provided in work-family programs complicates the business life for many middle managers. Their experience says that employees work five days a week, eight hours a day (at least). Further, the traditional "command and control" management style is still prevalent, that is, the supervisor is in a clear position of authority that includes monitoring the time spent by employees on the job. Flexible hours for employees are a significant change for managers and we need to help them with the training and encouragement to make work-family practices be successful. Unfortunately, some supervisors may never accept the changes. Some corporate cultures discourage employees from using work-family benefits such as flexible hours. Employees feel they may be viewed as not serious about work if they use such benefits and this would hurt their careers. Upper and middle management must communicate their support of work-family practices, and employees should use these practices.

Many middle managers also have family responsibilities and they can benefit from work-family programs. But the job flexibility that is such a strength of these programs may not be easy to apply for people in supervision roles. Every effort should be made to make work-family programs useful to all employees, including middle managers.

WORK-FAMILY PROGRAMS AT THE MARRIOTT CORPORATION

The Marriott Corp. is one example of an organization with an extensive program (they call their program Work/Life). Most Marriott locations operate 24 hours a day, seven days a week and have a complicated work schedule environment for both the business and the employees.

Marriott has a program of "Alternative Work Arrangements" to help their associates balance personal and professional responsibilities. These alternatives include flextime, compressed work week, reduced work week, telecommuting (work at home), and job sharing. Associates propose an alternative work arrangement and are given help in writing the proposal to recognize the effect on the business, customer, and associate.

Other Marriott programs encompass:

- Childcare

    - Childcare discount directory

    - Maternity matters – birth or adoption

    - Public policy work on childcare

- Eldercare

    - Eldercare locator

    - Elder relocation program

    - Discount at Marriott senior living services properties

- Education, training, and information

    - Management and supervisory training (on work/life management)

    - The Balance Newsletter (providing information on work/life issues, workplace effectiveness, and best practices)

    - Work/Life website

- Family Care Spending Account – Marriott associates who pay for childcare, eldercare, or care of a disabled family member can set aside tax-free money for these expenses.

- Marriott's Associate Resource Line – a toll-free 24 hours a day, seven days a week confidential program that offers consultation and referral on a wide range of work and personal life issues. The service is available in 150 languages. Additional programs include library-by-mail, tips on tape, volunteerism, College Level Exam Program (CLEP), and participation in the federally sponsored Earned Income/Advanced Income Tax Credit program to earn additional income.

Marriott recognizes that work-family issues also affect their managers. The "Management Flexibility" concept emphasizes getting the job done rather than the number of hours worked. Managers are required to identify inefficiencies and low-value work that may cause long hours. The process is called "work redesign" (the theme of this book).

Mariott's Management Flexibility concept reflects transforming attitudes and behaviors, changing hours, and redesigning processes. Here are some of their principles:

- Think hard about the way you do your work.

- Change your own behaviors (don't feel guilty and don't criticize others about leaving early).

- Communicate (positive reinforcement, discourage negative behavior).

- Foster teamwork (fill in for someone who needs to leave early).

- Constantly look at better ways to do things.

Their approach used these elements: a pilot process at three locations, have managers respond to surveys, hold focus groups to identify issues causing long hours, outline possible solutions to minimize inefficiencies, measure the impact of flexibility initiatives, and change attitude and behaviors toward work. Notice their focus on reducing work overload by studying and redesigning the work. At the pilot locations, hours were reduced by almost five hours per manager, low-value work was cut in half, managers report lower levels of stress and burnout, there is less emphasis on hours worked and more emphasis on important work accomplished, and management is more supportive of personal/family responsibilities. For a refreshingly frank paper on the Marriott experience, see Munck (2001).

This book aims to reduce work overload in two ways: 1) eliminate waste from processes and use the resources saved to reduce the work overload of the remaining activities, and 2) redesign work to reduce the mental demands that also contribute to work overload. When work overload is present, the resulting stress spills over into family life creating problems at home, which, in turn, affects employee performance back on the job – a vicious circle. Work-family programs of the type described in this chapter are wonderful. But work-family programs alone, or teaching employees how to handle job stress alone, cannot solve the problem of work overload. Thus, we must redesign processes to eliminate waste and redesign jobs to reduce mental demands.

SOURCES OF INFORMATION ON WORK FAMILY PROGRAMS

Information is conveniently available for you to learn the basic concepts – and to keep up to date – on work and family practices.
My suggestions are:

1. **Human Resources Institute**, affiliated with The University of Tampa. This organization does research in the broad area of human resource issues and practices. The Institute monitors more than 150 major issues including those in the work and family area. Over 100 companies support the Institute. The website – www.HRInstitute.info – is continuously updated.

2. **Families and Work Institute**. The Institute does "research that provides data to inform decision making on the changing workplace, changing family, and changing community." The Institute also receives support from companies. Their website is www.familiesandwork.org.

3. *Fortune* **magazine**. The annual issue on "100 Best Companies to Work For" provides a wealth of examples of specific practices by company.

4. *Working Mother* **magazine**. The annual issue on "100 Best Companies for Working Mothers" provides details on work-family practices, by company.

5. **Alliance of Work/Life Professionals**. This organization promotes a healthy balance between work and personal life. The website is www.awlp.org.

These sources have been a great help to me in doing research for this book.

SUMMARY – THREE KEY POINTS

1. For more than half of American families, jobs of the wage earners (one or more) now have a significant negative impact on family life.

2. Our ever-increasing desire for a higher standard of living causes burdens to add to family income, leading to work overload.

3. Many organizations demonstrate that work and family activities to help employees are feasible, but many other organizations do not respond to the need. To the laggards: it can be done, the evidence is crystal clear.

In the final chapter, we will sum it all up.

12

What Do We Do Next?

Some people believe that the current grey-haired generation "lives to work," but the younger generation X "works to live." Such generalizations have far too many exceptions to be useful. Work overload is a problem for many people.

After a recap, we will offer some immediate action steps by upper and middle management to launch the overload battle.

A RECAP

1. Many people do have work overload; many people do not have work overload. Middle managers and individual professional contributors (particularly those whose activities involve much customer contact) lead the overload brigade.

2. People who are suited and pleased with their jobs willingly handle (even enjoy) some excess hours (and even stress). But there is a limit.

3. The increased pace of work and family life feed on each other, that is, long work hours means less time for family and the fast pace of family activities adds mental and physical burdens to work.

4. Work overload leads to errors in work, safety risks, job dissatisfaction, and other serious issues.

5. People who experience work overload perceive the main reasons are insufficient resources, firefighting, work processes that are not capable, problems with internal and external suppliers, computer hardware or software problems, information overload, unclear performance goals and responsibilities, inadequate selection and training of personnel, and other reasons.

6. Most work processes include activities that contribute little or nothing to the final output. We know how to eliminate these waste activities from a process. By eliminating the waste, we can use the resources saved to reduce the work overload.

7. To reduce work overload, we must analyze both the technical content and the mental demands of the work. The components of mental demands are mental intensity, time spent on the job, content and authority, management support, career aspects, and social interaction. We can redesign the job for these mental demands.

8. Work redesign for the workforce should result in jobs of sufficient scope to provide for learning new skills. Participation of workers in planning the redesign and empowerment in decision making leads to a state of self-control for the workforce.

9. The matching of skills (inherent and acquired) and interests with job requirements is essential. More intense efforts to make a good match yield significant benefits.

10. To reduce and control work overload, the redesign of work activities should be the primary action to take. Upper management must provide the time and special skills necessary for redesign.

11. Methods to handle job stress can be an important supplement to redesign of work, but the work redesign is critical because it removes some sources of overload and therefore reduces the stress.

12. The workforce has permanently changed. Families are now in the workforce. For companies to obtain the best talent, the companies need work family programs.

SWING INTO ACTION

Throughout this book, I have suggested some actions for upper and middle management. This final chapter suggests a few immediate actions that could break the impasse on work overload. It won't be easy and there will be reasons why some of these actions won't work. So . . . we will state an action and then an obstacle of why the action won't work, and, finally, what we could try to overcome the obstacle. First, some actions for upper management.

WHAT SHOULD UPPER MANAGEMENT DO NEXT?

Action by Upper Management

Find out the extent of work overload.

This won't work because . . . We know work overload is a problem but it's infrequent, only happens to a few people, and the circumstances are beyond our control.

But maybe we could try . . . Ask accounting to add up the paid overtime hours for the past year and also the unexpended vacation time for middle managers and individual professional contributors. Also have the middle managers and professional contributors keep track of their (unpaid) overtime for a representative period of one month. If the results confirm that overload may be a serious problem then conduct a full study on the total cost of work overload. See Chapter 10 for details.

Action by Upper Management

Eliminate mandatory overtime.

This won't work because . . . Circumstances often make it necessary to have mandatory overtime.

But maybe we could try . . . As an experiment, eliminate mandatory overtime for say, three months, while simultaneously eliminating waste from processes. This means upper management must guarantee that the savings from eliminating waste will be used to reduce work overtime. See Chapter 10.

Action by Upper Management

Upper management should meet with upper management of another company that has an extensive work-family program to learn about the benefits.

This won't work because . . . Work-family issues are too different in various companies.

But maybe we could try . . . A one-time meeting – just a few hours – to hear from another CEO firsthand about the benefits and implementation ideas on work-family activities. See Chapter 11.

Now, some actions for middle management.

WHAT SHOULD MIDDLE MANAGEMENT DO NEXT?

Action by Middle Management

Keep a time log for one month recording time spent by simple categories such as departmental planning and administration, firefighting, personnel issues, meetings, managing information, business travel, or any set of appropriate categories. See Chapter 9.

This won't work because . . . This is unnecessary; I know where I spend my time.

But maybe we could try . . . Don't rely on your memory – get some data. Ask an assistant to keep the time log for you.

Action by Middle Management

As an experiment, study waste in two cross-functional processes.

This won't work because . . . We don't have the time or skills to do it.

But maybe we could try . . . The study could be done by a staff department, retirees, a consultant, students from a local college, or some other source. See Chapters 3 and 4.

Action by Middle Management

As an experiment, study two individual jobs for excessive mental demands due to job content or poor management systems.

This won't work because . . . We don't have the time or skills to do it.

But maybe we could try . . . Use the self-control checklists and other material in Chapter 6 to analyze the jobs. Ask for volunteers – a middle manager to guide the study and workers to participate with ideas. See Chapters 5 and 6.

A CLOSING NOTE

Capitalism has helped to make America great. Most of us want a capitalist society but not one that means work overload. As capitalists, we can be smart enough to solve the work overload problem.

We started this book with a reference to Frank and Lillian Gilbreth. The Gilbreths are watching us to see if we get it right on work overload.

That's all I have to say.

Appendix A

Can't We Act Tomorrow on Work Overload?

(See Chapter 9)

1. Eliminate mandatory overtime (to force the study of waste in processes).

2. Set a target date for eliminating the work overload.

3. Set up an employee roundtable to brainstorm ideas on how to ease the overload.

4. Hire temporary help.

5. Request "shared resources" temporarily from another department.

6. Give a person who just finished a high overload project a new temporary project that he or she personally enjoys, to partially overcome the suffering from the overload.

7. Identify and reduce excessive mental demands in key jobs.

8. Provide compensatory time off.

9. Add fun to the work.

10. Encourage people to do recovery/rejuvenation techniques every 90 to 120 minutes.

11. Pull out the stops on reward and recognition.

Appendix B

List of Actions by Middle Management

(See Chapters 9 and 12)

Basic: Devise ways to identify and eliminate waste from work processes and reduce excessive mental demands. As a pilot approach:

- Study waste in two cross-functional processes
- Study two individual jobs for excessive mental demands

Departmental planning and administration

Time management:

- Read a time management book
- Keep a time log of activities for a representative month
- Add 20 percent to time estimates for projects
- Schedule a half hour each day for assessing priorities

Setting priorities on major projects:

- Twice a year, step back and review current projects

Follow through on projects:

- Focus on a few goals
- Learn to say "no" to additional work
- Delegate
- Add fun to the job

– If overload cannot be eliminated quickly, have a plan of actions to compensate for the overload

Firefighting:

– Short-range actions

* Add temporary help

* Train additional firefighters

* Face the reality that some fires (problems) will not be solved

– Long-range action:

* Prevent the fires (see Chapter 10 under Long Range Actions)

Personnel Issues

- Recognize the symptoms of work overload
- Plan work to rejuvenate people after work overload
- Install an automatic follow-up on the status of open (unfilled) personnel requisitions
- Pursue additional sources of recruiting personnel
- Pursue approval of additional resources as part of a long-range strategy (Chapter 10)
- Clarify job responsibilities
- Select and match people to job requirements
- Train people for a full career
- Address career and other personnel problems

Meetings

- Consider alternatives to meetings
- Prepare thoroughly for meetings
- Conduct meetings efficiently
- Follow-up after meetings

Managing Information

- Review internal information received
- Drop subscriptions to some magazines
- Review how to handle e-mails
- Collect selected data (see six criteria in Chapter 9)

Business Travel

Alternatives:

- Videoconferencing
- Satellite broadcasting
- Teleconference calls
- Teleconference calls with data collaboration
- E-mail

Appendix C

List of Actions by Upper Management

(see Chapters 10 and 12)

Determine the extent of work overload

- Determine the costs of work overload.

- Have accounting assemble data on unexpended vacation time for middle managers and individual professional contributors.

- Have human resources audit departments to determine the extent of work overload for all personnel.

- Consider the impact of work overload on families.

- Ask upper and middle management what other information on work overload to collect.

- Consider using a consultant to study work overload.

Have some or all middle managers develop a strategy for work overload in their departments

- Define the operational goals for the department.

- Determine the current level of work overload and how this relates to bottom-line measures.

- Determine the key causes of work overload.

- Set goals, with time targets, on removing the causes.

- Develop and implement plans to achieve the goals of current work overload areas.

- Provide for a periodic review with upper management on progress toward meeting the goals.

- Set up controls to continuously manage work overload.

Operational actions by upper management

- Eliminate mandatory overtime.

- Meet with upper management in another company that has an extensive work-family program.

- Make clear to all that the total work hours must stay within reason.

- Provide resources to study processes for waste.

- Help middle managers to reduce their work overload.

- Make sure middle managers have sufficient time to periodically review priorities.

- Support middle managers on reducing excessive mental demands on all jobs.

- Support middle managers on matching jobs with people.

- Support middle managers on retention of key personnel.

- Search for creative solutions to work overload and tap the ideas of all personnel.

- Inject fun activities.

- Take compensating actions when work overload cannot be reduced.

- Achieve cooperation and teamwork among middle managers (five recommendations in Chapter 10).

Appendix D

Actions to Minimize Work Overload

(See Chapter 9)

- Decide where you want to go in life and make plans to get there.
- Don't forget the essentials: exercise, food, sleep, spiritual, time to do nothing.
- Set long-range and short-range work objectives.
- Avoid excessive emphasis on task completion (hurry sickness).
- Be a corporate athlete:
  - Physical capacity
  - Emotional capacity
  - Mental capacity
  - Spiritual capacity
  - Rituals and rejuvenation

Appendix E

Stress Reducing Techniques

(See Chapter 9)

Become aware that you are stressed

- Create a personal stress log to identify the types of situations that cause stress. The log should document the date, situation, intensity of the stress, and your thoughts and actions.

- Identify specific patterns of negative thinking and learn to substitute positive responses to block out the negative.

Apply relaxation techniques to induce relaxation to alleviate the stress and to prevent future stress

- Meditation – empty your mind of active thought, particularly negative thought.

- Progressive muscle relaxation – systematically relax muscle groups.

- Belly breathing (diaphragmatic breathing) - breathe slowly in and out through the nostrils.

- Guided imagery – create a favorite scene in your mind and use it to escape unpleasant situations (perhaps use an audio tape).

- Hypnosis and self-hypnosis – create a focused state of consciousness that helps you to enter a calm, meditative state.

- Biofeedback – use monitoring devices to furnish information about stress.

- Self-observation – to furnish information about stress.

Physical techniques

- Physical exercise.

- Yoga – a regimen of breath control, meditation, and stretching and strengthening exercises ending in meditation.

- Tai Chi – one form (called T'ai Chi Chih ®) is a series of 19 gentle movements and one pose that stimulates, circulates, and balances the energy in the body.

- Baths – warm, leisurely.

Social and spiritual support

- Social interaction – enjoy the company of your friends.

- Spirituality – personal prayer to help induce a meditative state and relaxation.

Work environment

- Music.

- Color and design of workplace.

Body essentials

- Proper diet.

- Sleep at least seven hours.

- Exercise.

Increase your tolerance level for stress

- Have clarity on job responsibility.

- Have a job with meaningful purpose.

- Have a job design that approaches self-control and avoids excessive mental demands.

- Have some fun and use other rituals to recover and rejuvenate.

Some excellent references on stress reduction and exercise

1. Harvard Health Publications. 2001. *Mind/Body Medicine,* Harvard Health Publications.

    This is a 41-page booklet prepared by the Harvard Medical School that interprets extensive medical information on stress for the general reader. The booklet provides a readable scientific explanation of how our minds affect our bodies, presents tools and techniques to use, and how all of this relates to relates to seven major health conditions. The booklet includes a glossary of medical terms, a list of organizations to contact for further information, and a selected list of books for further reading.

2. Potter, Beverly. 1998. *Overcoming Job Burnout – How to Renew Enthusiasm for Work.* (Berkeley, CA: Ronin Publishing, Inc.)

    This is a 302-page book written by a counseling psychologist that blends humanistic psychology and Eastern philosophies with the principles of behavior psychology. The book covers the causes of burnout and presents the principles of managing stress and how these can be applied to eliminate job burnout and make work life more meaningful. An extensive bibliography directs you to further reading.

3. National Institute on Aging. 2001. *Exercise.* (Gaithersburg, MD: U. S. Department of Health and Human Services). To order a free copy, call 800-222-2225.

    This is an 80-page booklet written by health scientists at the National Institutes of Health with advice from a distinguished group of health scientists from universities. The booklet covers four types of exercises: endurance, strength, balance, and flexibility. The step-by-step instructions for each type of exercise are super clear – even include diagrams. Every family should have this booklet.

References

Chapter 1

DeGraaf, John, David Wann, and Thomas H. Naylor 2002. *Affluenza – The all-consuming epidemic.* (San Francisco: Berrett-Koehler Publishers).

Galinsky, Ellen, Stacy S. Kim, and James T. Bond 2001. *Feeling overworked: When work becomes too much.* (New York: Families and Work Institute).

Munck, Bill 2001. Changing a culture of face time. *Harvard Business Review* (November): 125-131.

Rapoport, Rhona, Lottie Bailyn, Joyce K. Fletcher, and Bettye H. Pruitt 2002. *Beyond work – family balance.* (San Francisco: Jossey-Bass).

Reich, Robert B. 2001. *The future of success.* (New York: Alfred A. Knopf).

Chapter 2

None.

Chapter 3

AT&T Quality Steering Committee 1990. *Achieving customer satisfaction.* (Indianapolis, IN: AT&T Customer Information Center).

Damelio, Robert 1996. *The basics of process mapping.* (New York: Quality Resources).

Gryna, Frank M. 2001. *Quality planning and analysis,* fourth edition. (New York: McGraw-Hill).
Juran Institute Inc. 1980. *Quality improvement tools – flow diagrams.* (Wilton, CT: Juran Institute).

Chapter 4
Batson, Robert G., and Tracy K. Williams 1998. Process simulation in quality and BPR teams. *Annual Quality Congress Proceedings.* (Milwaukee: American Society for Quality): 368-374.
De Marco, Tom 2001. *Slack.* (New York: Broadway Books).
Fortune 1985. The Renaissance of American Quality (October 14).
Hammer, Michael, and James Champy 1993. *Reengineering the Corporation.* (New York: Harper Business).
Lawson, M.B. (Buff) 2001. In praise of slack: Time is of the essence. *Academy of Management Executive* 15, no. 3:125-135.
Nohria, N., and R. Gulati 1996. Is slack good or bad for innovation? *Academy of Management Journal* 39, no. 4: 1245-1264.

Chapter 5
Karasek, Robert, and Töres Theorell 1990. *Healthy work.* (New York: Basic Books).
Van Yperen, Nico W., and Mariëtt Hagedoorn 2003. Do high job demands increase intrinsic motivation or fatigue or both? The role of job control and job social support. *Academy of Management Journal* 46, no. 3: 339-348.

Chapter 6
Davis, Robert, Susan Rosegrant, and Michael Watkins 1995. Managing the link between measurement and compensation. *Quality Progress* (February): 101-106.
Friedman, Stewart D., Perry Christensen, and Jessica DeGroot 1998. Work and life – The end of the zero-sum game. *Harvard Business Review* (November-December): 119-129.
Gryna, Frank M. 2001. *Quality planning and analysis,* fourth edition. (New York: McGraw-Hill). Reproduced with permission of The McGraw-Hill Companies.
Hackman, J. Richard, and Greg R. Oldham 1980. *Work redesign.* (Reading, MA: Addison-Wesley Publishing Company).
Hemsath, David 2001. *301 more ways to have fun at work.* (San Francisco: Berrett-Koehler Publishers).
Karasek, Robert, and Töres Theorell 1990. *Healthy work.* (New York: Basic Books).

Shirley, Britt. M., and Frank M. Gryna 1998. Work Design for Self-Control in Financial Services. *Quality Progress* (May): 67-71. American Society for Quality, Reprinted with Permission.

Wallin, L., and I. Wright 1986. Psychosocial aspects of the work environment: A group approach. *Journal of Occupational Medicine* 28: 384-393.

Weinstein, Matt 1996. *Managing to have fun*. (New York: Simon & Schuster).

Wrzesniewski, Amy, and Jane E. Dutton 2001. Crafting a job: Revisioning employees as active crafters of their work, *Academy of Management Review* 26, no. 2: 179-201.

Yerkes, Leslie 2001. *Fun works creating places where people love to work*. (San Francisco: Berrett-Koehler Publishers).

Chapter 7

Gustafson, Carl 2001. Employee retention: Ways to maximize this competitive edge. *Sterling Conference*, Orlando.

Leonard, James F. 1986. Quality improvement in recruiting and employment. *Juran Report Number Six* (Winter). (Wilton, CT: Juran Institute Inc).

Levering, Robert, and Milton Moskowitz 2004. 100 best companies to work for. *Fortune* (January 12): 58-78.

Ligos, Melinda 2001. The company was downsized. Now you're upsized. *New York Times* (October 28): Money and Business Section 11

McDermott, Robin E. 1994. The human dynamics of total quality. *Annual Quality Congress Proceedings* (Milwaukee: American Society for Quality Control): 225-233.

Maslach, Christina, and Michael P. Leiter 1997. *The truth about burnout*. (San Francisco: Jossey–Bass).

Morgan, Ronald B., and Jack E. Smith 1996. *Staffing the new workplace*. (Milwaukee: ASQ Quality Press and Chicago: CCH Incorporated).

Reichheld, Frederick F. 2001. Lead for loyalty. *Harvard Business Review*, (July – August): 76-84.

Wood, Alfred 1994. Employee retention. *Manage* 46, no. 2: 4-7.

Chapter 8

Argyris, Chris 1998. Empowerment: The emperor's new clothes. *Harvard Business Review* (May – June): 98-105.

Aubrey, Charles A. II, and Derek S. Gryna 1991. Revolution through effective improvement projects. *Quality Congress Transactions.* (Milwaukee: American Society for Quality): 8-13.

Avery, Christopher, with Meri Aaron Walker and Erin O'Toole Murphy 2001. *Teamwork is an individual skill: Getting your work done when sharing responsibility.* (San Francisco: Berrett–Koehler Publishers).

Baker, Edward M. 1988. Managing Human Performance. In *Juran's Quality Control Handbook*, fourth edition. (New York: McGraw-Hill Book Company). Reproduced with permission of the McGraw-Hill Companies.

Centano, Ann, Karla Ahn, and Roberta Tawell 1995. Operation-alizing quality in daily work concepts. *Impro Conference Proceedings*, Juran Institute Inc.

Forrester, Russ 2000. Empowerment: Rejuvenating a potent idea. *Academy of Management Executive* 14, no.3: 67-80.

Fortune 2001. (September): 3, 206L.

Gryna, Frank M. 2001. *Quality planning and analysis*, fourth edition. (New York: McGraw-Hill).

Gryna, Frank M. 1981. *Quality circles.* (New York: AMACOM).

Harvard Business School 1994. Case 9-694-076 Taco Bell, Cambridge, MA.

Katzenbach, Jon R., and Douglas K. Smith 1993. *Wisdom of teams.* (Boston, MA: Harvard Business School Press).

Mann, David W. 1994. Re-Engineering the manager's role. *Annual Quality Congress Transactions.* (Milwaukee: American Society for Quality): 155-159.

Skiba, Karen D. 1996. Accelerated continuous improvement methodology. *Impro Conference Proceedings*, Juran Institute Inc.

Wetlaufer, Suzy 1999. Organizing for empowerment: An interview with AES's Roger Sant and Dennis Bakke. *Harvard Business Review* (January–February): 110-123.

Chapter 9
Aft, Lawrence S. 2000. *Work measurement and methods improvement.* (New York: John Wiley & Sons).

Benson, Herbert M.D., and William Proctor 2003. *The break-out principle.* (New York: Scribner).

Bohn, Roger 2000. Stop fighting fires. *Harvard Business Review* (July–August): 83-91.

Bruch, Heike, and Sumantra Ghoshal 2002. Beware the busy manager. *Harvard Business Review* (February): 62-69.

Drucker, Peter F. 2002. They're not employees, they're people. *Harvard Business Review* (February): 70-77.

Guernsey, Lisa 2001. Why e-mail is creating multiple e-personalities. *New York Times*, (September 26): Business and Technology Section 3.

Gunther, Marc 2001. God and Business. *Fortune* (July 9): 59-80.

Harmon, Amy 2001. Remote rendezvous, worried travelers warm up to videoconferencing, *New York Times*, (September 24): Business Section 1, 4.

Hartman, Bob 1983. Implementing quality improvement. *Juran Report Number Two*, Juran Institute Inc.: 124–131.

Harvard Health Publications 2001. *Mind and body medicine.* (Boston, MA: Harvard Health Publications).

Hindle, Tim 1998. *Manage your time.* (New York: DK Publishing, Inc.)

Hutchings, Patricia J. 2002. *Managing workplace chaos.* (New York: AMACOM).

Loehr, Jim, and Tony Schwartz 2001. The making of the corporate athlete. *Harvard Business Review* (January): 120-128.

Pfeffer, Jeffrey, and Robert I. Sutton 2000. *The knowing – doing gap.* (Boston, MA: Harvard Business School Press).

Smith, Gerald F. 1998. *Quality problem solving.* (Milwaukee: ASQ Quality Press).

St. James, Elaine 2001. *Simplify your work life.* (New York: Hyperion).

Ventrella, Scott 2001. *The power of positive thinking in business.* (New York: Simon and Schuster).

Weinstein, Matt 1996. *Managing to have fun.* (New York: Simon & Schuster).

Chapter 10

Bossidy, Larry, and Ram Charan 2002. *Execution.* (New York: Crown Business).

Gryna, Frank M. 2001. *Quality planning and analysis*, fourth edition. (New York: McGraw-Hill).

Kolb, Deborah M., and Judith Williams 2001. Breakthrough bargaining. *Harvard Business Review* (February): 89-97.

Longenecker, Clinton O., and Mitchell Neubert 2000. Barriers and gateways to management cooperation and teamwork. *Business Horizons:* 37-44.

RHI Management Resources 2001. *USA Today* (November 6): Bl.c.

Chapter 11

Bond, J.T., E. Galinsky, and J.E. Swanberg 1998. The 1997 national study of the changing workforce. (New York: Families and Work Institute).

Browning, Lynnley 2003. A burnout cure that few companies prescribe. *New York Times* (July 6) Money and Business Section 3: 7.

Doherty, William J., and Barbara Z. Carlson 2002. *Putting family first.* (New York: Henry Holt and Company, LLC).

Friedman, Stewart D., and Jeffrey H. Greenhaus 2000. *Work and family – allies or enemies?* (Oxford: Oxford University Press).

Munck, Bill 2001. Changing a culture of face time. *Harvard Business Review* (November): 125-131.

Reich, Robert B. 2001. *The future of success.* (New York: Alfred A. Knopf).

Rose, Karol 2003. Work life effectiveness. *Fortune.* (September 29): S1-S17.

Schor, Juliet B. 1992. *The overworked American.* (New York: Basic Books).

Working Mother magazine 2003. (October) Describes the 100 best companies for working mothers.

Chapter 12

None.

About the Author

FRANK M. GRYNA has degrees in industrial engineering and more than 50 years of experience in the managerial, technological, and statistical aspects of quality activities.

From 1991 to 1999, he served first as director of the Center for Quality and then as distinguished university professor of management at the University of Tampa. From 1982 to 1991, he was with the Juran Institute as senior vice president. Prior to 1982, Dr. Gryna was based at Bradley University, where he taught industrial engineering and served as acting dean of the College of Engineering and Technology. He is now distinguished professor of industrial engineering emeritus. Dr. Gryna was also assistant professor of statistical quality control at Rutgers University and served in the U.S. Army Signal Corps Engineering Labs. At the Space Systems Division of the Martin Company, he was manager of reliability and quality assurance.

In addition, he has been a consultant for many companies on all aspects of quality and reliability programs from initial design through field use.

He coauthored *Quality Planning and Analysis* with J.M. Juran and was associate editor of the second, third, and fourth editions of *Juran's Quality Handbook*. His research project, *Quality Circles*, received the Book of the Year Award sponsored by various publishers and the Institute of Industrial Engineers. He has received recognitions as a Fellow of the American Society for Quality, and a Fellow of the Institute of Industrial Engineers. He has also received various awards, including the Distinguished Service Medal, the Edwards

Medal, and the E. L. Grant Award of the American Society for Quality; Engineer of the Year Award of the Peoria Engineering Council; teaching and professional excellence awards; and the Award of Excellence of the Quality Control and Reliability Engineering Division of the Institute of Industrial Engineers. Dr. Gryna is also the recipient of the Ott Foundation Award, presented by the Metropolitan section of the American Society for Quality.

He currently does research and writing.

Index

Page references in italics indicate figures.

A

Abbott Laboratories, 170
absentees, 19
accidents, 8
acquisitions, 7
ACXIOM, 168
add on tasks, 3, 144
administrators, 50
    See also managers, middle;
        managers, upper
Adobe Systems, 89
adoption assistance, 169
AES Corporation, 99
affluenza, 7
AFLAC, 89, 168
Aft, Larry, 5, 115
Ahn, Karla, 101–2
Aid Association for Lutherans, 105
Alliance of Work/Life Professionals,
    171, 175
Alston & Bird, 89
American Century Investments, 166,
    169
American Express Consumer Card
    Group, 105
Amgen Corp., 168, 169
Amoco, 58
analysis
    of flow diagrams, 32, 33
    of job characteristics, 53–56
    of mental demands, 53–54
    of overload data, 143–44

personnel for, 24
of process data, 25–26, 30–33
for self-control, 53–54, 61–68
of waste, 25–33
Argyris, Chris, 100
artificial intelligence, 125
athletes, 132, 135, 136
AT&T, 116
Aubrey, Charles A., II, 100
audits, 23–24, 154
autonomy, 55
Avery, Christopher, 109

B

Bailyn, Lottie, 7
Baker, Edward M., 103
Baldwin, Bruce A., 131
Bank One Corporation, 92, 100, 108,
    147–48, 166, 169
Baptist Health Systems (South Florida),
    92
The Basics of Process Mapping (Damelio),
    32
baths, 194
Batson, Robert G., 37
Baxter Healthcare, 23–24, 96, 166, 170
belly breathing, 134, 193
benchmarking, 38, 42, 85, 146, 150–51,
    180
Benson, Herbert, 132
BF Goodrich Chemical Group, 103

biofeedback, 134, 194
black belts, 108–9
Blistex, 135
blitz teams, 101
Bond, James T., 4, 162
Booz Allen Hamilton, 170
boredom, 39, 46, 56
Bossidy, Larry, 154
bottlenecks, 40
boundaries of work processes, 25–26
boundary managers, 99
Bradley University, 24
brainstorming, 137
Bristol-Myers Squibb Co., 170
Browning, Lynnley, 169
Bruch, Heike, 117
budgets, 141
bullying, 3
bureaucratized service workers, 50
Bureau of Labor Statistics, 85, 162
burnout, 4, 44, 91, 148, 195
business travel, 127–28, 163, 187

C

capitalism, 181
career development/planning, 48, 49,
    59–60, 83, 90, 148
Carlson, Barbara Z., 165
Carter, Terry, 79
Catalytica Pharmaceuticals, 135
Caterpillar Tractor Co., 25
causes of work overload
    acquisitions, 7
    competitiveness among
        companies, 6
    computer problems, 14, 16–17, 113,
        120, 151, 178
    customer expectations, 7
    downsizing, 7, 88, 112, 147
    family activities, 7
    firefighting, 13, 14, 112, 178
    globalization, 6–7
    goals/responsibilities, unclear, 13,
        15, 113, 178
    information overload, 14, 16, 113,
        125, 178
    mergers, 7, 35, 49, 112, 147

resources, insufficient, 13, 14, 20, 112,
    151, 178
selection/training of personnel,
    inadequate, 14 (*see also* s
    election of personnel; training
    of employees)
standard of living, 7, 49, 90, 163, 164
supplier inputs, 14, 15–16, 113, 178
surveys to identify, 150
vital few, 151
work process control, lack of, 13, 15,
    112
work process inadequate to
    demands, 13, 15, 113, 151, 178
Census Bureau, 162
Centano, Ann, 101–2
chairs, 58
Champy, James, 36–37
change
    in job design, 74 (*see also* job
        redesigning)
    radical vs. incremental, 36–38
    resistance to, 141, 172
    timing of, 147
    See also redesigning work processes
Charan, Ram, 154
Charles Schwab, 169
Cheaper by the Dozen, 1
checklist for manufacturing sector,
    62–68
checklist for service sector, 68–75
Chick-fil-A, 80
childcare, 48, 49, 57, 60, 168
Christensen, Perry, 75
cognitive distortions, 134
colleges, as sources of analysis
    personnel, 24
commercialized service workers, 50
Commitment Flowdown™, 147–48
communication devices, 162
community relations, 171
commuting time, 162
competitiveness among companies, 6
computer modeling, 37
computer problems, 14, 16–17, 113, 120,
    151, 178
conflicts, 103
confrontation, fear of, 48
consultants, external, 24

Container Store, 89
contract workers, 123
control sequences, 155
cooperation, 157–58
costs, 8, 142–43, 146, 150
craftsmen, mental demands on, 50
credit unions, 87
critical thinking, 134
criticism, 3
cross-functional processes, 20, *21*
cross-functional/project teams, 24,
    100–101, 102, 104, 108, 144
Cummins Engine, 89
customers
    complaints from, 45, 55
    expectations of, 7
    external, 26, 27, 40
    identifying, 25–28
    internal, 26, 40
    needs of, discovering, 25–26, 28, 40,
        163
    prioritizing, 26–28, 156
    suppliers as, 26
    transferring activities to, 41

D

Damelio, Robert, 32
data
    analysis of, 143–44
    on extent/seriousness of overload,
        142–43, 146
    on retention, 91–92, 146
    selecting, 126–27
    work process, 25–26, 30–33
    See also measurement
Davis, Robert, 72
DeGraaf, John, 7
DeGroot, Jessica, 75
delegating authority/tasks, 98, 118, 185
Deloitte and Touché, 91
demand-control-support (DCS) model,
    50
DeMarco, Tom, 41
designing work processes. *See* redesign-
    ing work processes
desks, 58
diet, 132, 194
Dimon, Jamie, 148

disconnects, 30
Doherty, William J., 165
downsizing, 7, 88, 112, 147
dress codes, 58
Drucker, Peter F., 123
dual career ladder, 90
dust, 56
Dutton, Jane E., 56

E

Economic Policy Institute, 85
Edward Jones Company, 89, 168
efficiency, 1, 40–41
Eital, Tim, 83, 122, 128
eldercare, 48, 49, 57, 60, 168
Eli Lilly, 168, 170
e-mail, 16, 113, 124, 125–26, 128, 187
EMC, 168
emotional capacity, 132, 133–34
empathy, 148
employees
    borrowing of, 3, 19, 137, 144
    cost of losing, 89
    decision making by, 46–47, 55, 98
    finding, 84–88
    front-line, and customers, 8, 45, 55
    insufficient number of, 33
    jobs matched to, 79–83, 122, 157,
        178
    perceptions of being overloaded,
        4–5, 14
    rehiring of, 86
    relocation of, 168
    remote locations for, 87
    retaining, 89–92
    selection of, 14, 16, 64, 70, 80–84, *81*,
        113, 178
    skills of, and job content, 46–47,
        57–58, 178
    social interaction of, 45, 47, 58–59
    surveys of, 50
    tired, 3, 35, 148
    training of, 14, 16, 64, 70, 88–89, 93,
        113, 123, 178
    transportation for, 86
Employment Management Association,
    80
Employment Policy Foundation, 85

empowerment/participation, 48, 68,
  95–110, 178
  accountability arising from, 97–98
  definition/characterization of
    empowerment, 96–97
  fear of, 97–98
  and fear of job loss, 96
  guidelines for implementing, 98–99
  importance of, 97
  middle management's role, 99–100
  organizing work, 95–96
  ownership/responsibility
    arising from, 97
  salary increases arising from, 99
  and self-control, 100, 178
  and teams, 100–110 (*see also* teams)
  upper management's role, 99–100
  the workforce's role, 99–100
  workforce teams, 95
endorphins, 115
energy, 117–18
equipment, dangerous, 47
ergonomics, 47
errors, 177
  and injuries, 8
  inspections for, excessive, 22–23
  and productivity/costs, 8, 10
  rework to correct, 21–22
  by tired employees, 3
  vital few, identifying, 40–41
Esso Research and Engineering
  Company, 90
Ethicon Endo-Surgery, 58
exercise, 115, 130, 132, 134, 194, 195
Exercise (booklet), 195
exit interviews, 149
Exxon Mobil, 23–24

F

face time, 8
fairness, 48, 60
Families and Work Institute, 4, 7, 175
family. *See* work-family issues
Family and Medical Leave Act (1993),
  168
Fannie Mae, 170
fatigue, 50, 104, 136
fear, climate of, 95, 148

Federal Express, 166
feedback, 48, 55–56, 59, 65, 71–72
finance department, 23–24
financial compensation, 48, 49, 60, 90
firefighting
  by middle managers, 119–21, 186
  as a warning sign, 3
  as waste, 21
  work overload caused by, 13, 14, 112,
    178
First Tennessee Bank, 166
Fletcher, Joyce K., 7
flexible work options, 91, 166, *167*, 168,
  172
flextime, 46, 48, 49, 57, 60, 87, 157, 166,
  167, 172
flow diagrams
  nonvalue-added steps identified in,
    39
  for task identification, 54
  for work processes, 25–26, 27, 28–32,
    29, *32–33*
focus, 117–18, 134, 185
food services case study, 76
Ford Motor Company, 36–37, 58
Forrester, Russ, 100
Fortune, 88–89, 92, 96, 165, 175
Frank Russell, 169
Friedman, Stewart D., 75, 170
frustration, 8, 44, 53, 58, 103
Fry, Dolores, 59
fun, 58–59, 119, 137, 154, 157, 183, 185,
  195
Fun Works (Yerkes), 59

G

Galbraith, Kenneth, 141
Galinsky, Ellen, 4, 162
Gallup Organization Inc., 92
Gantt, Henry L., 105
gathering areas, 58
gender equity, 7
General Electric, 37
General Mills, 170
generational differences, 177
Ghoshal, Sumantra, 117
Gilbreth, Frank, 1, 23, 136
Gilbreth, Lillian, 1, 23, 105, 136

globalization, 6–7
goals, operational, 149
goals/responsibilities, unclear, 13, 15, 113
"God and Business" (Gunther), 135
Graniterock, 88–89
green belts, 108–9
Greenhaus, Jeffrey H., 170
Greyston Bakery, 135
Gryna, Derek S., 100
Gryna, Frank M., 62, 96, 100, 102, 106, 152, 163
Guernsey, Lisa, 126
guided imagery, 134, 193
Gulati, R., 41
Gunther, Marc, 135
Gustafson, Carl, 92

H

Hackman, J. Richard, 54
Hagedoorn, Mariëtt, 50
Hallmark, 169
hallways, 58
Hammer, Michael, 36–37
handoffs (white space), 40, 113
Harmon, Amy, 128
Hartman, Bob, 116
Harvard Business School, 105
Harvard Health Publications, 132, 195
hazards, 47, 56
health benefits/plans, 87, 166
health needs, 60
Hemsath, David, 59
Hewlett-Packard, 39, 58, 166
high performance model, 132–36
Hindle, Tim, 115
holidays, 119
Home Depot, 169
horizontal job enlargement, 54
hours
    flexible, 46, 48, 49, 57, 60, 87, 157, 166, *167*, 172
    increases in, 5–6, 35, 162–63
    keeping them reasonable, 156
    mental demands caused by, 44, 46, 121
humanists, 109
human resources department, 23, 92, 143

Human Resources Institute (University of Tampa), 175
humor, 119
"100 Best Companies to Work For" (*Fortune*), 88–89, 92, 165, 175
hurry sickness, 131
Hutchings, Patricia J., 131, 136
hypnosis, 134, 193

I

IBM, 37, 90, 170
IE. *See* industrial engineering
illness, 3
industrial democracy, 109
industrial engineering (IE), 1, 23, 32, 136
inefficiency, 40–41
information management, 125–27, 186–87
information overload, 14, 16, 113, 125, 178
information technology (IT), 16–17, 39–40, 87–88
injuries, 8
inspections, excessive, 22–23
International Labor Organization (United Nations), 5
internships, 86
interruptions, 3, 45
intimidation, 3, 148
isolation, 58
IT. *See* information technology

J

J.M. Smucker, 89
Job Content Questionnaire, 50
job redesigning, 53–77
    ability/desire to regulate the process, 65–68
    autonomy, 55
    career planning, 59–60
    checklist for manufacturing sector, 62–68
    checklist for service sector, 68–75
    control in doing the job, 58
    family-friendly practices, 60–61
    feedback, 55–56, 59
    job characteristics, analysis of, 53–56

and job content, 57–58
knowledge of what one is
        actually doing, 64–65, 70–72
knowledge of what one supposed is
        to do, 62–64, 68–70
management support, 59
mental demands, analysis of, 53–54
mental intensity of the job, 56
self-control, analysis for, 53–54,
        61–68
skill variety, 54, 56, 57
social interaction on the job, 58–59
task identity, 54–55, 56
task significance, 55, 56
time spent on the job, 57
work environment, 53
for work/family, 75–77
jobs
control in doing, 45, 47, 50, 58
descriptions of, 82
employees matched to, 79–83, 122,
        157, 178
meaningfulness of, 46–47, 54, 56
mental intensity of, 44, 45–46, 56, 178
rotation of, 89
security/lock-in, 48, 49
shared, 57, 166
social interaction on, 45, 47, 58–59,
        178
time spent on, 44–45, 46, 57, 178
working environment, 47, 57–58
See also job redesigning; job
        satisfaction
job satisfaction, 17, 177
and career development, 83, 90
and job content, 83
key elements of, 89–90
and narrow jobs, combining, 39
reductions in, 8
and repetitive sequences, 39
See also job redesigning
journals, 16
Juran, J. M., 61
Juran Institute, 31

K

Kaiser Permanente, 101–2
Karasek, Robert, 44, 50, 60–61
Katzenbach, Jon R., 109

Kim, Stacy S., 4
Klepfer, Jeffrey, 5, 44
knowledge processes, 41
knowledge workers, 123
Kodak, 86
Kolb, Deborah H., 147
Kritsas, John, 91

L

labor budgets, 141
laborers, mental demands on, 50
labor information, 85
lattice career paths, 90
Lawson, M. B., 41
lawsuits regarding overtime, 3
leadership teams, 144
Leiter, Michael P., 91
Leonard, James F., 85
letters, 16
Levering, Robert, 89
lighting, 58
Ligos, Melinda, 88
line of invisibility, 30
Loehr, Jim, 132
Long, Clayton, 136
Longenecker, Clinton O., 157–58
lunch at one's desk, 132
Lyons, Judith, 24, 123, 146

M

management practices
command and control, 172
mental demands caused by, 48–50,
        148
and waste, 33
managers, middle, 111–38
actions to be taken by, 137–38,
        180–81, 183, 185–89
bossy, 114
business travel by, 127–28, 187
care and well being of, 131–36
cooperation among, 157–58
delegating authority/tasks by, 98,
        118, 185
empowerment feared by, 97, 114
empowerment/participation role of,
        99–100

family responsibilities of, 131–32
firefighting by, 119–21, 186
focus/energy of, 117–18, 134, 185
and fun, 119, 157, 185
goals/objectives of, 130–31
identity of, 112
information managed by, 125–27,
186–87
meetings held by, 124–25, 186
mental demands on, 45–46, 50, 57
palliative actions by, 119, 157
people problems handled by, 79–80
personnel issues for, 121–24, 186
planning/administration by, 115–19,
185
prioritizing of projects by, 116–17,
147–48, 185
reductions in, 112
as suffering from work overload, 2
and teams, 102, 104, 106–7, 113–14
time spent on activities, 114–15, 123,
180
turnover among, 8
and upper managers, 117–18,
143–44, 156–57
vacation time for, 143
and work-family programs, 172
work overload of, 130–31, 177
managers, upper, 139–59
actions to be taken by, 156–58,
179–80, 189–90
change resisted by, 141, 172
convincing them of the problem,
141–43, 150–51, 179, 189
convincing them to act, 145–47, 150,
179
empowerment/participation role of,
99–100
extremes in, 139, 158
issues to be considered by, 147–49
leadership demands on, 139–40
mental demands on, 50, 57
and middle managers, 117–18,
143–44, 156–57
priorities of, 145–46
process analysis authorized by, 25
proposals/presentations to, 146–47,
155
reviews with, 154
salaries of, 60, 90
work overload of, 1–2, 177

Managing to Have Fun (Weinstein), 59
Mann, David W., 99
manufacturing sector checklist, 62–68
marginal workers, 50
marketing, 163
Marriott Corporation, 8, 22, 164, 169,
172–74
Maslach, Christina, 91
master black belts, 108–9
Mayo healthcare system, 101
Mazda, 36
MBNA America Bank, 168, 169
McDermott, Robin E., 82
McDonald's, 86
measurement
and audits, 154
guidelines, 125–27, 155
on retention, 91–92
of work processes, 25–26, 30
See also data
medical leave, 60, 168–69
meditation, 130, 134, 135, 193, 194
meetings, 124–25, 186
memos, 16
mental capacity, 132, 133, 134
mental demands, 43–51, 137, 157
analysis of, 53–54
control in doing the job, 45, 47, 50, 58
and job content, 44–47, 57–58, 178
and long hours, 44, 46
and management practices, 48–50,
148
mental intensity of the job, 44, 45–46,
56, 178
by occupation, 50
social interaction on the job, 45, 47,
58–59, 178
time spent on the job, 44–45, 46, 57,
178
mental health needs, 169
mentoring, 87
mergers, 7, 35, 49, 112, 147
Met Life, 168
micromanaging, 148
Microsoft Office, 40
middle managers. *See* managers, middle
Mind and Body Medicine (MBM report),
132–35, 195
moonlighting, 7
Morgan, Ronald B., 82, 84, 90
Moskowitz, Milton, 89

mothers, working, 5, 49, 162, 170
motivation, 50, 91
Munck, Bill, 8, 174
Murphy, Erin O'Toole, 109
muscle relaxation, 134, 193
music, 194
Myers-Briggs Type Indicator, 82

N

National Enterprise Operations Division
    (Bank One),
    147–48
National Institute on Aging, 195
National Workplace Bullying Advice
    Line (UK), 3
Naylor, Thomas H., 7
negative thinking/emotions, 103,
    133–34, 193
negotiating, 147
net conferencing, 127
Neubert, Mitchell, 157–58
Nike, 169
Nohria, N., 41
noise levels, 47, 56, 57
nonvalue-added steps, 22, 39
"no," saying, 118, 185

O

occupational groups, 50
Oldham, Greg R., 54
"100 Best Companies to Work For"
    (*Fortune*), 88–89, 92, 165, 175
operational goals, 149
organization boundary, 30
Orion Advisory, LLC, 147–48
outside actions, 41–42
outsourcing, 86–87, 123
Overcoming Job Burnout (Potter), 195
overtime, 3, 46, 57, 60, 137, 169, 179, 183
The Overworked American (Schor), 163

P

Pacific Bell, 87
palliative actions, 119, 157
Pareto principle, 31, 40–41, 150–51

Pareto priority index (PPI), 116–17
participation. *See* empowerment/
    participation
participative management, 109
part-time workers, 122, 166
pastoral care, 87
Paychex, 89
Peale, Norman Vincent, 135
people. See employees
people building, 109
    See also empowerment/
        participation
people with disabilities, 86
personality, 81–82
personal priorities. *See* work-family
    issues
personnel. *See* employees
personnel requisitions, 84–88, 122, 141,
    150–51
Pfeffer, Jeffrey, 127
pharmaceutical plant case study, 75–76
physical capacity, 132–33
Pitney Bowes, 58
planning/administration, 115–19, 185
Plan Vista Solutions, 123
pollution, 47
Pontiac Motor, 102
position descriptions, 82
positive thinking, 134, 135
Potter, Beverly, 195
power naps, 132
The Power of Positive Thinking (Peale),
    135
*The Power of Positive Thinking in
    Business* (Ventrella), 135
PPI (Pareto priority index), 116–17
primary processes, 20
prioritizing of projects, 116–17, 147–48,
    185
prison labor, 86
problems
    handling, 74–75
    prioritizing, 121
    sporadic vs. chronic, 119–20
    See also firefighting
procedures, clarity/completeness of,
    63, 69
processes. See work processes
process maps, 26
    See also flow diagrams

procrastination, 118
Proctor, William, 132
productivity, 8, 10
products, prioritizing, 156
professional contributors
    care and well being of, 131–36
    identity of, 128–29
    vacation time for, 143
    work overload of, 130–31
professional employee
        organizations (PEOs), 123
professionals, mental demands on, 50
project-by-project approach, 152–55,
    171–72
project teams. See cross-functional/
    project teams
proposals/presentations, 146–47, 155
proverbs
    Arrogance diminishes wisdom, 48
    Don't overwork a willing horse, 6
    A good example is half a sermon,
      165
    Habit is a shirt that we wear until
      we die, 39
    He who commences many things
      finishes but few, 148
    He who stumbles over the same
      stone deserves to break his
      neck, 31
    If your friend is made of wax, don't
      place him near the fire, 57
    It is too late to come with the water
      when the house is burned
      down, 121
    A small hole can sink a big ship,
      17
    Soft words don't scratch the tongue,
      108
    Talk doesn't cook rice, 91
Prudential Financial Inc., 170
Pruitt, Bettye H., 7
purpose, sense of, 135

Q

quality culture, 67–68, 75, 96
quality department, 23
Quality Planning and Analysis (Gryna),
    96, 152, 163

R

Rapoport, Rhona, 7
Raymond James Financial, 81, 83, 91,
    122, 128
recognition, 48, 60, 91, 103, 138, 183
recovery events, 135–36, 138, 183,
    195
recruiting, 80, 85–86, 87–88, 186
    See also selection of personnel
redesigning work processes
    to eliminate waste, 35–36, 156
    guidelines, *38*, 38–42
    need for, 25–26, 34
    outside actions, 41–42
    process inefficiencies, 40–41
    process planning, 40
    radical vs. incremental change,
      36–38
    and time/resources, 41
    types of design changes, 35–36
    and work content, *38*, 39–40
reengineering, 36–37
Reich, Robert B., 162, 164, 165, 168
Reichheld, Frederick F., 80
rejuvenation, 122, 135–36, 138, 183, 186,
    195
relaxation, 130, 134, 135, 193–94
Republic Bancorp, 89
resources
    insufficient, 13, 14, 20, 44, 112, 151,
      178
    slack, 41
    and waste elimination, 20, 25
respect, 48, 81–82, 102–3
responsibilities, understanding of, 58
retirees, 86
retirement planning, 169
reviews of work, 64–65, 70–72
rewards, 48, 60, 103, 138, 183
rework, 21–22, 31, 32
rituals, 135–36, 138, 183, 195
Ritz-Carlton Hotel Company,
    105
Rivera, Andy, 119
Rogen International, 126
Rogers Corp., 85
Rose, Karol, 169
Rosegrant, Susan, 72
routinized workers, 50

S

S. C. Johnson & Son, Inc., 170
salaries, 60, 90, 99
sales revenue, 96
SAS Institute, 89
satellite broadcasting, 127–28, 187
Schor, Juliet, 163
Schwartz, Tony, 132
Sears, 82, 124
selection of personnel, 14, 16, 64, 70,
    80–84, *81*, 113, 178
self-control, 53–54, 61–68, 100, 178
self-hypnosis, 134, 193
self-managing teams, 101, 104–8
self-respect, 102
Servicemaster Co., 86–87, 135
service sector checklist, 68–75
shareholders, 172
shifts for work, 19, 35, 162
Shirley, Britt. M., 62
shopping, love of, 163
Silver, Larry, 81
single-parent households, 162
situational leadership, 109
Six Sigma, 23, 108–9
Skiba, Karen D., 101
skill variety, 54, 56, 57, 88–89
slack, 41
sleep, 130, 132, 194
Smith, Douglas K., 109, 121
Smith, Jack E., 82, 84, 90
social capital, 109
social interaction, 45, 47, 58–59, 178, 194
social support, 135
software, 39–40
    See also computer modeling;
        computer problems
Southwest Airlines, 80
specialists, career development/salaries
    of, 90
spiritual capacity, 132, 133, 135
spiritual support, 194
sports, family participation in, 164
St. James, Elaine, 131
stakeholders, 26
    See also customers
standard of living, 7, 49, 90, 163, 164
standards, 63, 66–67, 69–70, 72–74
Starbucks, 166

Steelcase, 58
strategy, development of, 149–55, 189–90
stress
    childcare/eldercare as a source of, 57
    definition, 4
    managing/reducing, 19–20, 132,
        136–37, 178, 183, 193–95
    mental demands as producing, 44
    sources, 4, 8, 11, 136
    See also mental demands
students, 24, 85–86
suggestion programs, 103
supervisors, 102–3
    See also managers, middle
suppliers
as customers, 26
inputs from, 14, 15–16, 113, 178
transferring activities to, 41
surveys of employee opinions, 92
Sutton, Robert I., 127
Swanberg, J. E., 162
symptoms of work overload, 3–4, 121

T

Tai Chi, 194
task identity/significance, 54–55, 56
Taylor, Frederick W., 104–5
TD Industries, 89
teams, 100–110
    blitz, 101
    cross-functional/project, 24, 100–101,
        102, 104, 108, 144
    effectiveness of, 108–9
    effects on employees, 102–4
    facilitators of, 108–9, 124–25
    importance of, 110
    leadership, 144
    management's support of, 102, 106
        (*see also under* managers,
        middle)
    self-managing, 101, 104–8
    workforce, 95, 101–4, 106, 114
    work space for, 58
technicians, mental demands on, 50
technology
    for boring jobs, 46, 56
    and customer expectations, 7
    and job security, 49

and work hours, 162
See also specific technologies
telecommuting, 87, 166
teleconferencing, 128, 187
telephone calls, 16
temperature levels, 47, 57
temporary help, 121, 123, 137, 183, 186
Texas Instruments, 90
Theorell, Töres, 44, 50, 60–61
threats, 3
301 More Ways to Have Fun at Work
(Hemsath), 59
3M, 90
time estimates for processes, 41, 185
Time Inc., 169
time management, 115, 134, 185
Tawell, Roberta, 101–2
training of employees, 14, 16, 64, 70,
88–89, 93, 113, 123, 178
transfers, 83, 122–23
travel, business, 127–28, 163, 187
trust, 48, 107
turnover, 8, 91, 148

U

Ultimate Home Care, 59
upper managers. *See* managers, upper
urgent vs. important projects, 116

V

vacation time, 3
value stream maps, 26, 28
See also flow diagrams
Vanguard Group, 169
Van Yperen, Nico W., 50
variation, minimizing, 67
Ventrella, Scott, 135
vertical job enlargement, 55
videoconferencing, 127, 187
Vista Plan Solutions, 24, 146
Volvo Cars, 60–61

W

Waan, David, 7
Wachovia Corporation, 170

Walker, Meri Aaron, 109
Wallin, L., 60–61
warning signs of work overload, 3–4,
121
waste
amount of, 20
analysis of, 25–33
eliminating, 20, 25 (*see also* redesigning work processes)
firefighting, 21
frustration as, 44
inspections, excessive, 22–23
and management practices, 33
monetary savings from eliminating,
171–72
nonvalue-added steps, 22
resources, and elimination of, 20, 25
rework to correct errors, 21–22
unnecessary steps, 22
Watkins, Michael, 72
web conferencing/link, 127
Wegmans Food Markets, 89
weight control, 132
Weinstein, Matt, 59, 119
welfare to work programs, 86
Wetlaufer, Suzy, 99
white space (handoffs), 40, 113
Williams, Bob, 5–6, 137
Williams, Judith, 147
Williams, Tracy K., 37
Woodward Governor, 102
workaholics, 147
work content, *38*, 39–40
work environment, 47, 56, 57–58, 66,
103, 194
work-family issues, 161–76, 169
changes in, 162–63, 178
childcare, 48, 49, 57, 60, 168
demographic facts, 162, 171
eldercare, 48, 49, 57, 60, 168
family activities, 7, 164
family-friendly practices, 48, 49–50,
60–61, 148, 165–69
family leave, 60, 168–69
gender equity, 7
and job redesigning, 75–77
loss of family time, 162
medical leave, 60, 168–69
overtime, 169 (*see also* overtime)
pace of family life, 164–65, 177

simplicity, 164
See also work-family programs
work-family programs, 49
  benefits of, 170–71, 178, 180
  information sources on, 175
  instituting, 171–72
  at Marriott Corporation, 172–74
  and middle managers, 172
  services included, 168–69
  top companies, 170
workforce teams, 95, 101–4, 106, 114
work groups, self-regulating, 48
work hours. *See* hours
Working Mother, 170, 175
work overload, overview of
  actions to minimize, summary, 191
  causes, 6–7 (*see also* causes of work
     overload)
  complaining, 6
  consequences, 8
  immediate steps to take, 137–38, 183
  people affected, 1–2, 11
  scope of the problem, 4–6, 34,
     142–43, 179
  self-assessment, 9–10
  viewpoints, 10–11
  warning signs, 3–4, 121
work processes, 19–34
  adjusting, 67
  analyses of, personnel for, 23–25
  boundaries, defining, 25–26
  causes of problems in, 31
  changing work vs. people, 19–20
  control, lack of, 13, 15

and customers, 25–28
data analysis, 25–26, 30–33
definition, 20
flow diagrams for, 25–26, 27, 28–32,
   29, 32–33
inadequate to demands, 13, 15, 31,
   113, 151
vs. jobs, 34
maintaining, 67
and management practices, 33
measuring, 25–26, 30
and performance standards, 66–67,
   72–74
types, 20, *21*
waste in, amount of, 20
waste in, analysis steps for, 25–33
waste in, forms of, 21–23
See also redesigning work processes
work sampling, 115
work shifts, 19, 35
workweek length. *See* hours
Wright, I., 60–61
Wrzesniewski, Amy, 56

X

  Xilinx, 89

Y

  Yerkes, Leslie, 59
  yoga, 194